THE BEGINNING
OF POLITICS

THE BEGINNING
OF POLITICS

Power in the Biblical Book of Samuel

_____

MOSHE HALBERTAL
AND STEPHEN HOLMES

PRINCETON UNIVERSITY PRESS
PRINCETON AND OXFORD

Library of Congress Cataloging-in-Publication Data

Names: Halbertal, Moshe, author. | Holmes,
Stephen, 1948– author.
Title: The beginning of politics : power in the biblical Book of
Samuel / Moshe Halbertal and Stephen Holmes.
Description: Princeton : Princeton University Press, [2017] |
Includes bibliographical references and index.
Identifiers: LCCN 2016050190 | ISBN 9780691174624
(acid-free paper)
Subjects: LCSH: Bible. Samuel—Criticism, interpretation, etc. |
Power (Social sciences)—Biblical teaching. | Politics in the Bible.
Classification: LCC BS1325.6.P6 H35 2017 |
DDC 222/.406—dc23 LC record available at
https://lccn.loc.gov/2016050190

British Library Cataloging-in-Publication Data is available
This book has been composed in Sabon LT Std
Printed on acid-free paper. ∞
Printed in the United States of America
1 3 5 7 9 10 8 6 4 2

TO TOBY PERL FREILICH
AND TO THE MEMORY
OF AMOS ELON

Contents

Acknowledgments

The main ideas of this book were developed in a joint seminar we taught on the Book of Samuel at the NYU School of Law. We also benefited greatly from presenting a chapter of the book at the Law School's always lively faculty seminar. Thanks go to our students and colleagues for their many stimulating insights and comments. The writing of the book was supported by grants from the New York University School of Law's Filomen D'Agostino and Max E. Greenberg Research Fund.

We are deeply grateful to colleagues and friends who offered us their wisdom, criticism, and support. The perceptive reactions and suggestions of David Cohen, Jon Elster, Tom Geoghegan, Roni Goldstein, Annette Hochstein, Ken Jowitt, Job Jindo, Diana Lipton, Vivian Liska, Marcia Pally, Illana Pardes, Dan Pekarsky, Amélie Rorty, and the anonymous readers for Princeton University Press were most helpful. We especially wish to express our gratitude to Toby Perl Freilich and Gloria Origgi for their contribution to the formation of the ideas of the book and their wonderfully meticulous comments on the manuscript.

Finally, we are grateful to Fred Appel, our editor at Princeton University Press, for his unfailing encouragement and thoughtful advice.

A Note on Text and Translation

Among the various English language renditions of the Book of Samuel, we have chosen to use Robert Alter's translation, published originally as *The David Story* (1999). We have followed as well Alter's reconstruction of the biblical text, opting among the textual variants presented by the Masoretic version, the Qumran scrolls, and the Septuagint. We have gained a great deal not only from the masterfully illuminating quality of his translation, but also from Alter's running commentary which, among its other virtues, is attuned to the political dimensions of the narrative that are at the center of our exploration. Our analysis also covers the first two chapters of the Book of Kings, recounting David's last days, chapters that scholars rightfully consider to be a continuation and conclusion of the story of David presented in the Book of Samuel and that stem from the hand of the same author.

THE BEGINNING
OF POLITICS

Introduction

THE EMERGENCE OF POLITICS

The literary qualities of the Book of Samuel are rightfully considered among the supreme achievements of biblical literature.[1] It is no exaggeration to say that the author of Samuel produced what is still the best book ever written in the Hebrew language. But alongside his genius as a storyteller, this anonymous author was also an uncannily astute observer of politics and the complexities of power.[2] What makes his book not only a literary masterpiece but also a profound work of political thought is the way in which the beautifully crafted narratives cut to the core of human politics, bringing into relief deep structural themes that transcend the particular events and fates of the book's main protagonists and that remain resonant wherever and whenever political power is at stake. This dimension of the author's achievement, which is what makes Samuel such a penetrating and endlessly fertile exploration of political life, will be our principal focus in this book.

We part company, as a consequence, with the many gifted biblical scholars who have interpreted the Book of Samuel as a political text with partisan aims. Such scholarship has long debated whether the book is pro-David or anti-David, and whether its source was among Saul's surviving loyalists or instead among proponents of a strictly antimonarchical ideology. In our opinion, these debates, while interesting and important in their own right, can distract from the book's theoretical significance. Because the author, as we hope to show, remains rather critical of all sides and does not paint a flattering portrait of any of the work's principal characters, it is impossible, in our view, to pin down the party or faction that the book is meant to endorse. This quandary has led to two results in the scholarship. Some scholars have ascribed the text to a variety of authors. When the partisan outlook changes, they argue, a promonarchical author has replaced an antimonarchical one or vice versa, or a pro-Davidic voice has been supplanted by an anti-Davidic source.[3] This multiple-author hypothesis, which assumes that clashing political manifestos are stitched together in the surviving text, fails to do justice, we believe, to the unity and brilliance of the authorial voice connecting many of the book's narratives. Another group of scholars, by contrast, has attributed the narratives of the Book of Samuel more or less to a single authorial voice while speculating, for example, that an ambiguous portrait of David might actually serve as an apology for his conduct.[4] Our focus is different. In order to concentrate on the trenchant understanding of power woven consciously and deftly into the narrative, we have done our best to free the text from questions such as whether it defends or attacks David and which contemporary faction it was composed to flatter or support.

In fact, the Book of Samuel does not display a one-sided allegiance to any of the political factions that competed for power at the time. Its author didn't write a political book, therefore, but rather a book *about* politics. Every reading of a work this rich is destined to be tentative and partial, and ours is certainly no exception. But by liberating the Book of Samuel from the search for a partisan agenda and by focusing instead on its copious insights into the nature of political power in general, we hope to shed at least some new light on its outstanding brilliance and originality.

We have not attempted to write a biography of David. Nor have we surveyed the ways David has been portrayed in subsequent literature and art.[5] Rather than offering character studies of Saul and David, we emphasize the author's searching look into the effects of sovereign power on those who wield it, trying to tease out what the book implies, for example, about the way the newly emergent institution of hereditary monarchy shaped the motivations as well as the actions of Israel's first two kings. Our book does have a hero, of course. But this hero is not one of the protagonists of the Book of Samuel, be it David or Saul. Our hero is rather the author of this magnificently imagined history of Saul and David's sequential reigns, an author-hero who shines through his insights into the complex workings of political power.

The prestige and authority of the Bible in general and the Book of Samuel in particular have inspired numerous readers, past and present, to seek the origins of modern Western political ideas, including republicanism and egalitarianism, in the ancient biblical tradition.[6] We have not joined this worthwhile search for precursors of modern moral ideals in the political culture of an ancient kingdom. We have chosen instead to concentrate on the fine-grained phenomenology of political power so astutely elaborated by our anonymous author. What makes the book so alive to the touch even today are not its normative teachings, if any, but rather its analysis of political power, an analysis that we believe to apply not only here and now but whenever and wherever structures of power exist.[7]

Such a rich and subtle grasp of politics finds few antecedents in the literature of the ancient Near East or in biblical literature prior to the Book of Samuel. Unlike other dimensions of biblical religion, the book's relentlessly observant and critical gaze into the dynamics of power was neither an elaboration on, nor a repudiation of, themes and concerns present in the myths and narratives of Israel's neighbors.[8] In the Book of Samuel we hear a fresh and original voice. It is not merely the earliest extant document of its kind but arguably the earliest ever written, and one that exhibits a startling maturity of insight. When first encountering its prescient grasp of political reality, one immediately realizes that the stories the text graphically recounts are anything but initial tentative steps in an inchoate thought process awaiting a more sophisticated elaboration and refinement. Rather, the book's insights into the dynamics of power contested, gained, abused, and lost possess that rare clarity, completeness, and depth that can probably be achieved only at a moment of origin, that is, only when a new reality bursts forth in a way that cannot be repeated. Even today, the book rivets its readers with an overwhelming sense of revelation. It conveys something utterly new and unprecedented.

Spectacular acts of human creativity can never be fully explained as products of their historical context.[9] But our author's insights into politics were made possible—though not necessary—by a revolutionary transformation in biblical political theology. A dramatic shift opened up new conceptual and experiential space within which the book's original perspective on political reality was able to emerge and develop. This theological shift and its inner logic is reflected and elucidated in the book itself, which not only introduced a new way of talking about power, but also dramatized the conditions that made such a novel way of speaking and thinking possible. It will be useful to preface our discussion, therefore, with an analysis of this prior momentous shift in political theology and the new space it opened up, always taking our lead from the way in which the author of the Book of Samuel presented both.

In the political theology typical of the great land powers surrounding ancient Israel, the king was either a God, an incarnation of a God, or a semi-mythic human king who was elected by the gods to serve as a necessary mediator between the divine order and the human world. Though there was certainly a spectrum of monarchic ideologies in the ancient Near East, kingship was not generally perceived as a historical institution that was consciously chosen at a certain critical moment in time out of the imperatives of communal life and in full recognition of the onerous burdens of taxation and conscription that would inevitably be imposed by a human sovereign as the price of organizing collective defense.[10] Elsewhere, for the most part, monarchy was understood as part of the permanent furniture of the cosmos itself. The legitimacy of monarchy, in such cases, depended more on the mythic order than on events unfolding in historical time.[11] In the ancient Near East, broadly speaking, the king not only governed the political community but, as a semicosmic force, played a crucial role in maintaining the order of nature itself. He did this in his ritually performed priestly role. In the canonized scribal accounts of the ancient Near Eastern kings and their deeds, the deification of kingship and general veneration of political authority meant that an unblinking look into the moral trespasses, ambiguous virtues, and personal shortcomings of monarchs and emperors was exceedingly rare.[12]

The biblical political theology that preceded the dramatic events recounted in the Book of Samuel upended this ancient Near Eastern formula. Rather than declaring that "the king is a God," the new theology postulated instead that "God is the king." The sole or exclusive kingship of God was fundamentally irreconcilable with a consolidated political monarchy. The kingship of God entailed, as we see in the biblical Book of Judges, a divine monopoly on sovereign authority that essentially precluded the creation of self-sustaining political institutions.[13] In line with this new and revolutionary political theology stipulating the exclusive kingship of God, the period described in the Book of Judges was populated by heroic leaders of a special type, men who arose intermittently as charismatic saviors to deliver the Israelite tribes temporarily from their oppressors.

Such warrior-chieftains did not wield the two powers that classically define political sovereignty, namely the powers to draft and to tax. They materialized suddenly, as God-sent deliverers intervening in a violent, turbulent, and lawless historical scene without any kind of traditional legitimacy or prior planning and preparation. They summoned the tribes to follow them into battle while, for the most part, inspiring a negligible minority of genuine followers whose battlefield cohesion could not survive the leader's death.[14] According to the Book of Judges, God's miraculous presence in history was manifested not only in his periodically fielding such leader-saviors, but also in promoting their possible successes. In this pre-Samuel period, not only was no standing army established, but no enduring unity of purpose or centralization of political-military power was achieved or enforced.[15]

Such a divinely inspired "savior style" of crisis leadership precluded the creation of a reliable, politically organized continuity of power. In such a context, no single stable ruler capable of asserting his supreme authority over tribes and clans that were often embroiled in blood feuds could emerge. But the enduring existence of a supreme authority is the most elemental underpinning of any human political order. This is because leaderless interregna will inevitably invite attacks by foreign enemies and spark violent succession struggles, civil wars, or even a shattering of the community. Such tangible dangers associated with political power vacuums explain why all political entities aim first and foremost to organize a smooth transfer of power from one leader to the next, with no gaps and no violent factional contestation. Dynastic monarchy offers one possible solution to the problem of regime continuity in a dangerous and unpredictable world. Through the bloodline of the king's family, hopes for a nonviolent transfer of power may just possibly be fulfilled.

The unqualified rejection of dynastic succession in the Book of Judges was echoed in God's direct political rule as apotheosized in the revolutionary new theology of "God is the king." Hostility to hereditary kingship was powerfully expressed in Gideon's answer to the men of Israel who longed for monarchy and the continuity of political sovereignty that monarchy seemed to promise: "And the men of Israel said, 'Rule over us, you and also your son and also your son's son, for you have rescued us from the hand of Midian.' And Gideon said to them, 'I will not rule over you nor will my son rule over you. The LORD will rule over you'" (Judges 8:22–23). From the perspective of the pre-Samuel political theology of the Book of Judges, then, the absence of a widely accepted supreme ruler in the interval between one leader and the next was no vacuum at all. It was filled by the everlasting presence of God, the one true king.

Although the new political theology implied by "God is the king" was radically opposed to the traditional political theology that still dominated most contemporary political communities in the surrounding Near East, it too discouraged a probing and unsqueamishly critical examination of the ruling power. Human politics in the full sense of the word did not and could not exist in such a state of divinely supervised anarchy, a weak political order in which factious tribes were only tenuously knit together by a shared religious cult administered by territorially dispersed prophets and priests.[16] Although God the sovereign was sometimes disobeyed, he was certainly no subject for systematic critical scrutiny and political analysis.

The conditions for the emergence of genuine *political* thought, as a result, were established only when a third alternative emerged between these two radically opposed outlooks, between "the king is a God" and "God is the king." The first part of the Book of Samuel narrates, among other events, a dramatic break from God's direct sovereignty over political events. This is the essence of the shift from "God is the king" to "the king is not a God." That theological change allowed for the establishment and recognition of purely human sovereignty which, in turn, gave birth to a vividly insightful way of thinking and speaking about the newly emergent and self-sustaining political reality.

In the Samuel narrative, both the shift away from the political theology of the Book of Judges and the initial appearance of monarchy in Israel are presented as events occurring in human history. They do not belong to the mythic past. The biblical king, enthroned before our eyes, is a thoroughly human being, not a God. He is not a pillar of the cosmic order. He plays a negligible and wholly dispensable role in religious ritual, does not convey divine commands to his people, does not maintain the order of nature, and is not the prime lawgiver.

Admittedly, mythical conceptions of monarchy are not entirely absent from the biblical material. The royal hymns in the Book of Psalms (chapters 2, 45, and 110), for example, offer striking examples of a political theology very similar to that of other communities in the ancient Near East.[17] Yet the Book of Samuel reflects a radically different conception. For one thing, monarchy is described as emerging rather late in the history of Israel. It arose under emergency conditions, from the worldly needs of a rickety confederation of tribes that, at this particular moment, were seeking protection from the better-armed and better-trained Philistines—a new and threatening enemy nation that had dealt them one defeat after another. To the Israelites, pressed by an aggressive and militarily superior adversary, God the king seemed absent and remote. The people therefore yearned for a human sovereign able to muster and command a visible standing army, a worldly sovereign who could marshal and coerce them into a coordinated military response to a lethally powerful external foe.[18] They demanded that Samuel, the last of the judges, establish a dynastic monarchy to ensure continuity of sovereignty over all Israel through the bloodline of a king. The monarchy for which they were pleading would thus answer the people's two most pressing and existential political concerns: the need for unity and the need for continuity. In this telling of the worldly founding of biblical kingship, the people, united by consanguinity and their covenant with God, preceded the monarchy and caused it to be instituted. The kingship was not a mythic force, therefore, but rather an institution that was voluntarily embraced for strategic reasons in historical time. Its emergence reflected the people's incapacity or refusal to keep faith with the radical theological notion of God's exclusive kingship when faced with the threat of extinction or enslavement by a mighty foreign army.

Samuel, ancient Israel's last premonarchical leader, having planned for his own wayward children to succeed him in the role of prophet and judge, was mortally offended by the people's request for a worldly king. He felt personally rejected:

> And it happened when Samuel grew old that he set his sons up as judges for Israel. And the name of his firstborn son was Joel and the name of his second born was Abijah—judges in Beersheba. But his sons did not go in his ways and they were bent on gain and took bribes and twisted justice. And all the elders of Israel assembled and came to Samuel at Ramah. And they said to him, "Look, you yourself have grown old and your sons have not gone in your ways. So now, set over us a king to rule us, like all the nations." And the thing was evil in Samuel's eyes when they said, "Give us a king to rule us." And Samuel prayed to the LORD. And the LORD said to Samuel, "Heed the voice of the people in all that they say to you, for it is not you they have cast aside but Me they have cast aside from reigning over them. Like all the deeds they have done from the day I brought them up from Egypt to this day, forsaking Me and serving other gods, even so they do as well to you." (1 Sam 8:1–5)

Wallowing in a sense of personal betrayal, Samuel failed to perceive the larger and more momentous turning away implicit in the people's demand for a worldly king. God needed to remind Samuel that what was at stake was the kingship of God himself, and that in the people's request for a king like all the other nations, God the king was being popularly dethroned. Earlier in Israel's history, Gideon was faced with the same demand by the people, and he dismissively replied that kingship was an exclusive attribute of God, nontransferable to human beings. Any attempt to establish a human monarch was therefore idolatrous, since idolatry is the transfer of attributes and gestures that are exclusive to God to other beings. It is no wonder that God himself, in his words to Samuel, experienced the new request as yet another example of his people forsaking him in order to worship other gods.

Elsewhere in biblical literature, such an idolatrous violation of divine exclusivity would naturally provoke God's anger and jealousy. At this point, therefore, we might have expected a harsh denunciation by God of the people and their implicitly idolatrous plea for a human king. And yet God, in a startling act of self-limitation, abdicated his monopoly on the throne. By commanding Samuel to fulfill the people's request, God renounced his exclusive supremacy in the political domain. It is as if God understood that the worldly and especially the military consequences of his monopolistic claim to kingship, which implicitly denied the possibility of a self-sustaining political sphere, were simply too punishing for the people to bear. For a precarious community surviving in an unforgiving environment, the vacuum that opened in the intervals between episodic savior-leaders, and the incapacity of such transient chieftains to impose unity of action on a flimsy, fractious tribal confederation or to establish a standing organized force during their occasional appearances, created conditions of ultimate political anxiety that made God's direct kingship untenable. God had to readjust to human expectations. In so doing, he relinquished what had been his exclusive claim on sovereignty, thereby exculpating human kingship from the charge of idolatry. Between the collapse of the utopian ideology of God's kingship on the one hand and the refusal to deify the king on the other, a semiautonomous sphere of human politics was born. God is not the king, and the king will be accepted only so long as he renounces all claims to be a god.

Although magnanimous, in a way, God's remarkable renunciation of kingship was by no means free of a residual bitterness. This bitterness is essential to the basic attitude of the author of the Book of Samuel toward the human political sphere. It permeates the book's systematically ambivalent perspective on politics as a sphere of action indispensable to the material and spiritual survival of human communities but also originating in a troubling and haunting compromise. With a lingering sense of betrayal, God instructed Samuel not only to yield to the elders' and the people's demand for a king like all the other nations, but also to "solemnly warn them and tell them the practice of the king that will reign over them" (1 Sam 8:9). Samuel's catalog of the king's onerous privileges, proclaimed at the very moment when the unified Israelite polity came into being, introduces the reader to the fundamentally problematic nature of mankind's political project. For one thing, if the sovereign amasses enough power to provide security for the people against their enemies, he will also be strong enough to threaten and oppress the people he is supposed to protect. Indeed, the very act of organizing the people for self-defense inescapably involves a painful degree of tyrannical subordination, resource-extraction, and unfreedom.

These were the privileges of any worldly king as Samuel bitingly listed them to the people following God's request:

> And Samuel said all the words of the LORD to the people who were asking of him a king. And he said, "This will be the practice of the king who will reign over you: Your sons he will take and set for *himself* in his chariots and in *his* cavalry, and some will run before *his* chariots. He will set for himself captains of thousands and captains of fifties, to plow *his* ground and reap *his* harvest and to make *his* implements of war and the implements of *his* chariots. And your daughters he will take as confectioners and cooks and bakers. And your best fields and your vineyards and your olive trees he will take and give to *his* servants. And your seed crops and your vineyards he will tithe and give to *his* courtiers and to *his* servants. And your best male and female slaves and your cattle and your donkeys he will take and use for *his* tasks. Your flocks he will tithe, and as for you, you will become *his* slaves." (1 Sam 8:10–17, italics added)

In this passage, Samuel states the obvious about worldly kings. They possess the privilege to tax, which means to confiscate their subjects' property, and to draft, which means the right to enlist able-bodied young men in the army whether they wish to serve or not. These immense extractive powers are constitutive aspects of any political sovereignty, be it a monarchy or a liberal state. Without them, there can be no defense against predatory enemies. And yet, for all the good these powers can achieve, they are also very likely to be redirected toward purposes unrelated to a people's own safety and well-being. The critical tone informing the recitation of this stock list is subtly conveyed by Samuel's repetitive use of the third-person singular. The king will exploit these privileges for *his* wars, *his* chariots, *his* fields.[19] The manpower and property he will extract from his people will not necessarily be put to use as efficient instruments for the protection of the common good by defensive wars. Rather, the powers that are presumably granted to the monarchy for collective purposes may well be commandeered to serve his personal or dynastic interests. While pursuing his own glory, the king and his immediate loyal entourage will be sorely tempted to enslave the very people whom the monarchy was allegedly established to defend from being enslaved by enemy powers.

The people made their choice with full knowledge, after ample warning. They did not accept and celebrate worldly monarchy in a bout of absentmindedness, naively unaware of its toilsome burdens and trade-offs. They reasoned that subordination to a king was better than conquest by an enemy. As a result, God, who has been betrayed and in response has willingly resigned his monopoly on kingship, warns the people that he is not going to intervene on their behalf. "And you will cry out on that day before your king whom you chose for yourselves and he will not answer you on that day" (1 Sam 8:18). The people will be left to their own devices. They will be granted political autonomy, allowed or compelled to pay the price of their choice after having been duly informed of the consequences. God's self-removal from the political sphere is therefore dramatic and consequential, if not definitive or complete. Though God did not seek to punish the people when acceding to their request for him to relinquish his monopoly, his refusal to intervene at that moment of crisis indirectly set the naturalistic machinery of punishment in motion. This is what it means to deny that God's self-limitation was unreservedly magnanimous. It left a rueful residue of misgiving behind.

Neither Samuel's warnings about the king's inevitable abuse of royal privileges nor God's threat to refrain from coming to the people's rescue when they fully understand the suffering inflicted by their king was enough to overcome the people's acute anxiety about the lethal consequences of the breakdown of political authority in the intervals between successive savior-leaders. Single-minded in their desire to bridge these perilous stretches of leaderless anarchy between charismatic saviors, the people disregarded Samuel's warning: "And the people refused to heed Samuel's voice and they said, 'No! A king there will be over us! And we, too, shall be like all the nations and our king will rule us and go out before us and fight *our* battles'" (1 Sam 8:19–20, italics added). Inverting Samuel's emphasis on the third-person singular, the people resort to the first-person plural, insisting that the king will fight "our battles."

At the heart of politics lies an existential urge for physical security, and the people proved willing and even eager to relinquish whatever unsupervised freedom and entitlements they enjoyed in the state of divine anarchy, and to surrender to a political sovereign who will freely tax and conscript them so long as he can also safeguard them from their pitiless enemies. Sovereignty does not emerge in the Samuel narrative out of a Hobbesian state of nature, therefore. It does not arise out of an imaginary war of all against all, but rather out of a historical state, realistically described as a weak confederation of frequently feuding tribes where political and military power was fragmented, intermittent, and dispersed. Although sharing a common religious bond, the various Israelite tribes had been unable to achieve unity and stability. They clashed repeatedly among themselves and were increasingly vulnerable to attacks from outside forces. The constituent building blocks of a proposed united kingdom, therefore, were not atomistic individuals but extended families or tribes.

In describing what is lost as well as what is gained in unifying the Israelite tribes under a single dynastic monarch, the Book of Samuel provides us with our earliest account of the arduous, contested, and historically contingent emergence of this-worldly sovereignty. The centralization of political-military authority is admittedly accompanied by priestly anointment and bestowed by the grace of God. But as will become evident as the narrative unfolds, sovereign authority is actually consolidated much less sacramentally, through a hard-fought struggle, by tactically ingenious applications of force and fraud deployed to overcome considerable human resistance.

To summarize: A thoroughly human and demythologized political sphere emerged in a space that had been opened between the two basic alternatives that characterized much of the ancient Near East and the prior biblical tradition. That purely human political domain constituted the baseline condition that made possible the book's distinctive voice and its unblinkingly observant and critical perspective on human politics. In its richly detailed account of this pivotal political breakthrough, the Book of Samuel infused the moment of origin with a deep ambivalence. The narrative notoriously lacks the celebratory features that usually accompany any coronation or heroic founding of a new political regime. Instead, this moment of origin is starkly colored by Samuel's, and especially God's, resentment. The pervasive shadow of divine resentment is what differentiates the all-too-human world of biblical politics from a cloudlessly secular or "disenchanted" realm. Our author is acutely aware of the troubles and tragedies of the political endeavor on the one hand and of its irresistible necessity on the other. The entire book is marked by a refusal to shield its readers from this excruciating but truthful ambivalence.

As our exploration widens and deepens, we will address a series of deep puzzles that the Book of Samuel presents. From which point of view, if not that of a political partisan, is the book written? Is the author an insider to politics or an outsider? Is he someone from the court or at its margin? What was the vantage point from which such an astonishingly original book could have been produced?

God has to find his place within the new dispensation as a retired king who is no longer active in his role and who is one of Samuel's characters. Though God threatened to become fully removed and inaccessible, in fact, as we shall see, he continued to be involved at every stage of political life, although his mode of intervention changed dramatically from the time when he was the king. The exploration of this transformation, which among other things permits the emergence of an autonomously human political realm, is one of the Book of Samuel's main concerns and achievements. The author does not exactly tell the story from God's point of view, admittedly. Yet the book was certainly fueled and inspired by what the narrator imagined to be God's viewpoint. When trying to convey God's perspective on the establishment of human sovereignty in the form of dynastic monarchy, the author employed the following tone: *I did not recommend that decision. It wasn't the initial plan I had for you. Human kingship was your choice, which you insisted upon even after being warned. You wanted it and I couldn't refuse you. So let us see how it unfolds, and what it means. And what will be my place in it.* God's ambivalence toward the political realm permeates the book with its nuanced and exploratory yet smolderingly critical force. Precisely because of its uncomfortable ambivalence, therefore, the Book of Samuel sets forth the proper attitude that should be assumed toward the political project as a whole. Illuminated from this systematically ambivalent stance, politics is seen as an overpowering human necessity that can never fully escape a potentially self-defeating betrayal at its very core.

Our author graphically portrays the acute insecurity at the origins of sovereignty. Yet he also formulates with unrivaled clarity the problematic essence of the human political project. He articulates these twin insights while giving an account of the emergence of the purely human political space that accompanied the replacement of one political theology by another, a revolutionary change that did not pass without leaving visible scars. In providing this unflinching account of political origins, our author also positions himself and his reader as skeptical observers of the dynamics of human power. His warily mistrustful perspective sharpens his vision. It allows him to give one of the most penetrating accounts ever written of the internal workings of human politics.

In analyzing Samuel's view of politics and the way in which its author unearthed and elucidated structural concerns that permeate the political endeavor, we do not strictly follow the chronological order of the book and its narrative. Instead, we examine sequentially a constellation of specific themes developed in the book and that are woven into some of the most dramatic moments in its narrative. As we explore each of these themes in turn, we carefully attend to the exquisite details of the narrative; our larger themes are embedded in these details, subtly and inextricably.

ONE

The Grip of Power

Our author's initial and arguably most striking revelation concerning power is that the paramount aim of those who successfully attain supreme authority is often reduced to nothing more exalted or idealistic than staying in power. This obsessional fixation on the means and trappings of power, independent of the greater or lesser purposes it can serve, defines not only the psychic life of many of those who exercise great political power, but also the way in which politics is institutionally structured to sustain and secure the ruler's privileges and capacities. Whenever retaining hold on high office, rather than realizing an ideological vision or implementing a political program, becomes the dominant aim of politics, sovereign power becomes for its wielder an end in itself, even while being publicly justified as a means for providing collective security. Although power is always justified to subjects as a means of repelling foreign conquest and attaining other collective goods, for the one who exercises it, sovereign power may easily turn into something desired for its own sake. This inversion of a means into an end, all too common in modern as well as archaic politics, causes another inversion in turn. As power becomes an end for a sovereign clinging desperately to it, other intrinsically worthy ends turn into disposable means. Rulers who wield their authority in the service of power as an end in itself regularly convert such ends as love, loyalty, the sacred, and moral obligation into mere means for eliminating dangerous rivals and staving off the loss of power, a loss that they morbidly dread.

Instrumentalizing such inherently valuable ends and turning them into mere means has a further fateful consequence for human politics. Since sovereigns are always able, and often tempted, to turn morality into an instrument, their observable actions become chronically ambiguous. Observers of such sovereign actions find themselves in perennial doubt as to their genuineness. Is the moral justification adduced by the wielder of power a mere pretext covering a purely self-serving political motivation, or is the action principled and driven by a moral quest? As our author details with exceptional subtlety, the irresolvable ambiguities of political action and passion are rooted in the deeply enigmatic and hugely consequential relation between public justification and private motivation. Although—and indeed because—the instrumentalization of morality is pervasive in political life, the political and the moral are thoroughly intertwined in ways in which even the sovereign himself cannot always disentangle. The exploration of these interconnected themes— the double reversal of turning means into ends and ends into means that lies at the heart of politics and the resulting ambiguity of political action—runs through much of the Book of Samuel, but it initially comes into focus as our author meticulously examines the corrosive impact of the psychological and political imperative to retain power on the life of Saul, the first king and the first genuine political figure known to the Bible.

I

Saul makes his first appearance in the chapter that follows the request of Israel for a king and God's initially indignant and ultimately resigned acquiescence. Introduced as the son of Kish from the tribe of Benjamin, Saul is described as "a fine and goodly young fellow, and no man of the Israelites was goodlier than he, head and shoulders taller than all the people" (1 Sam 9:2). Saul had the physical stature of a leader, but the sequence of events that follows makes clear that he was anything but an ambitious young man craving power and political authority. It is no accident that the narrative of Saul's journey away from home—a journey that leads to his anointment by Samuel as the future king—began with Saul seeking something trivial; he was sent by his father with one of his lads to retrieve some lost asses. After searching a large terrain and failing to locate the asses, Saul exhibited a sensitivity and uncertainty incompatible with crassly cynical ambition or a burning lust for power. He addressed the accompanying lad: "Come, let us turn back, lest my father cease worrying about the asses and worry about us" (1 Sam 9:5–6). Saul was a considerate and decent son, worrying about his father's worrying. So the lad, his inferior, took the lead, making sure that the quest did not end prematurely: "Look, pray, there is a man of God in this town, and the man is esteemed—whatever he says will surely come to pass. Now then, let us go there. Perhaps he will tell us of our way on which we have gone" (1 Sam 9:6–7). Drawing a sharp contrast between Saul's irresolution and his lad's initiative, our narrator has Saul voice an additional worry: "But look, if we are to go, what shall we bring to the man? For the bread is gone from our kits and there is no gift to bring to the man of God. What do we have?" And the lad answers: "Look, I happen to have at hand a quarter of a shekel of silver that I can give to the man of God, that he may tell us our way" (1 Sam 9:7–8). Not Saul but the lad carried the cash that could be offered to the man of God (who happened to be Samuel), and Saul merely followed his lead.[1] Although tapped to become king, Saul is artfully portrayed as the diametrical opposite of a political schemer consumed by naked ambition. Before acceding to the throne, he bears absolutely no psychological resemblance to the voracious monarchs whose insatiable craving for ever-greater power at the expense of their people's well-being was the subject of Samuel's prophetic warnings.[2]

Saul did not covet power. Power coveted him. Stung by what he apparently felt was a personal betrayal, Samuel initially took no action to fulfill the people's demand for a king. Indeed, a hapless Saul, singled out for the throne by God, had to be brought before the prophet: "At this time tomorrow," God said to Samuel, "I will send to you a man from the region of Benjamin and you shall anoint him prince over My people Israel" (1 Sam 9:16). Approaching Samuel for oracular help in tracking down the missing asses, Saul was stunned by Samuel's suggestion that what he had found instead was the hereditary kingship: "And as to the asses that have been lost to you now three days, pay them no heed, for they have been found. And whose is all the treasure of Israel? Is it not for you and all your father's house?" (1 Sam 9:20). Saul responded in character with wholly unfeigned modesty: "Am I not a Benjaminite, from the smallest of the tribes of Israel, and my clan is the least of all the tribe of Benjamin? So why have you spoken to me in this fashion?" (1 Sam 9:21). Disregarding this palpably sincere protest, Samuel proceeded to anoint the hitherto ambitionless Saul.[3] Samuel then demonstrated his prophetic gifts by accurately foretelling events that will occur soon thereafter, thereby convincing Saul that he was indeed destined to become Israel's first king.

Staged without witnesses on the outskirts of town, the clandestine anointment of Saul by Samuel is followed in the narrative by a public coronation at Mizpah, which again serves to underscore Saul's natural reluctance to assume the power that has been so unexpectedly thrust upon him. In the presence of all the people, a divinatory procedure was enacted in the form of casting a lot meant to reveal the monarch already selected by God. The lot fell first on the tribe of Benjamin, and then on the clan of Matrit, and finally, from among that clan, the lot fell on Saul. After the identity of the new king was thus made known, a strangely embarrassing moment ensued. Saul, the chosen one, couldn't be located: "and they sought him but he was not to be found" (1 Sam 10:22). When he was discovered at last hiding among the gear, the people dragged Saul to a kingship that he had unequivocally never sought for himself:

> And they ran and fetched him from there, and he stood forth amidst the people, and he was head and shoulders taller than all the people. And Samuel said to all the people, "Have you seen whom the LORD has chosen? For there is none like him in all the people." And all the people shouted and said, "Long live the king!" (1 Sam 10:23–24).

In this oddly graceless coronation ceremony, distinguished by Samuel's residual resentment and Saul's embarrassingly humble demeanor, a handsome but ambitionless king-designate was grudgingly enthroned.

Unlike someone long preparing to assume power, Saul didn't move swiftly to exploit the momentum of his coronation and consolidate his authority. The public gathering at Mizpah ended in anticlimactic dispersal: "Samuel sent all the people away to their homes. And Saul, too, returned to his home in Gibeah, and the stalwart fellows whose hearts God had touched went with him" (1 Sam 10:26–27). It is no wonder that Saul's slinking back into private life was followed with words of derision spat out by some skeptical and oppositional voices among the people: "And worthless fellows had said, 'How will this one deliver us?' And they spurned him and brought him no tribute, but he pretended to keep his peace" (1 Sam 10:27). But why exactly does the author of Samuel make sure that we see Saul as wholly devoid of lofty ambition and craving for power? It is sometimes said that the only one who can be trusted with power is the one who doesn't seek it. Yet our author, in these passages, obviously wished to convey a diametrically contrary thought. The account of Saul's first two coronations prepares us to see how the intoxicating appeal of supreme power will overtake even a character as naturally uncalculating, unassuming, and unenterprising as Saul.

The real establishment of Saul's authority and the emergence of a structure that resembles a permanent and concentrated political force capable of taxation and conscription occurred through neither clandestine anointment nor public coronation, but only after a decisive victory in war. As told in 1 Samuel 11, the Ammonite king Nahash offered a humiliating pact to the people of Jabesh-gilead, who were situated at the easternmost and therefore highly exposed margins of Israel's tribal settlements. The proposed pact included the gouging out of the right eye of each of the men of Jabesh-gilead, marking their defeat and subjugation in a permanent and visible facial defect that also rendered them unfit for military self-defense. Messengers from the city of Jabesh-gilead were urgently dispatched to Saul's residence at Gibeah to plead for reinforcements. Saul, the newly selected but still reticent king, hadn't yet assumed leadership. He was still working the land as a private farmer:

> And, look, Saul was coming in behind the oxen from the field, and Saul said, "What is the matter with the people that they are weeping?" And they recounted to him the words of the men of Jabesh. And the spirit of God seized Saul when he heard these words, and he was greatly incensed. And he took a yoke of oxen and hacked them to pieces and sent them through all the territory of Israel by the hand of messengers, saying, "Whoever does not come out after Saul and after Samuel, thus will be done to his oxen!" And the fear of the LORD fell on the people, and they came out as one man. (1 Sam 11:5–7)

Meant to humiliate all Israel, the Ammonite king's proposal roused Saul from his retreat into private life, dramatically overcoming his residual disinclination to exercise the royal office to which he had been raised. Acting in a way reminiscent of the charismatic ad hoc leaders portrayed in the Book of Judges, Saul's

call for arms, including his threat to destroy the economic liveli-
hood of any community within the Israelite federation that failed
to send troops to lift the siege of Jabesh-gilead, was spectacu-
larly successful, leading him to an utter rout of the Ammonites.

Writing about a world where battle-hardened tribes fought
for exclusive control of fertile land, the author of Samuel was
well aware that decisive victory in war is the most effective way
of establishing political legitimacy. Following Saul's victory we
are told: "And the people said to Saul, 'Whoever said, "Saul shall
not be king over us," give us these men and we shall put them
to death.' And Saul said, 'No man shall be put to death this day,
for today the LORD has wrought deliverance in Israel'" (1 Sam
11:12–13). This was the moment when Saul began to act like a
king. He established a permanent court with a small standing
army; he would no longer be found plowing his fields. Military
victory gave him a taste for power and the confidence to assume it. Even the hesitant and ambivalent Samuel was swayed
by Saul's success in war. In the wake of victory, the prophet initiated a third coronation,[4] this time wholeheartedly accepted by
the people and by Saul himself:

> And Samuel said to the people, "Come, let us go to Gilgal and
> we shall renew there the kingship." And all the people went
> to Gilgal and they made Saul King there before the LORD at
> Gilgal, and they sacrificed their communion sacrifices before
> the LORD, and Saul rejoiced there, and all the men of Israel
> with him, very greatly. (1 Sam 11:15)

From this point forward, the author of the Book of Samuel will
turn his penetrating gaze to the radically transformed inner life
of the originally unassuming and modest person who first had
power thrust upon him and only afterwards was seized by the
power that had descended upon him unsought.

Whether attained by craft or by chance, great power has a
way of defining the person who wields it. Finding themselves
venerated by those around them, the supremely powerful almost

inevitably begin to worship themselves. Once such intoxicating superiority is tasted, relinquishing it can be experienced as an obliteration of the self. This is especially true for an office that can be bequeathed to one's heirs, a promise or expectation that gives its present occupant an intimation of immortality. Even Samuel—the boy with no dynastic pedigree, who was born to a barren woman as gift of God, and who was brought to the center of leadership as a challenge to a corrupt dynastic priesthood—displayed fierce resistance to the loss of great hereditary power. In his old age, Samuel wished his sons to inherit his leadership role even though they were plainly unworthy. He felt personally betrayed by the people who rejected his sons. And he was seemingly forced by God to anoint a king against his will. Despite Saul's initial victories over the Ammonites and other tribal enemies of Israel, Samuel continued to resent the king he had anointed, and his seething resentment will inflict continuous blows on Saul until the very end. Though Samuel had witnessed firsthand Saul's personal reluctance and innocence, he couldn't resist treating Saul as an illegitimate usurper of his own role and power. A young and inexperienced king was destined to make mistakes. And Samuel, as we will see, did more than his share in pushing Saul to, and over, the brink.

Besides providing a telling and astute commentary on the complex role of religion in stabilizing and destabilizing political authority, the trap that Samuel arguably laid for Saul in order to undermine his confidence in the future also lets us glimpse the particularly problematic form of instrumentalization that will play such a prominent role in the narrative to come. Following Saul's first and clandestine coronation, we are told that Samuel commanded Saul to wait at Gilgal for seven days until he arrived to officiate over a burnt offering to God.[5] The narrator is careful not to say that this command was God's. It was initiated by Samuel, presumably motivated by his desire to be in charge and to ritually validate the properly hierarchical relation between himself and the new king. In the meantime, the Philistines were mustering for war, and Saul, who had enlisted the people of Israel, was waiting with increasing impatience for Samuel, whose delayed arrival was encouraging rampant desertion among the soldiers. Desertion was to be expected, as forces who are gathered for war but who do not engage tend to disperse. But it also reflected Saul's tenuous authority over an incompletely unified tribal confederation. As time passed, Saul's army shrank to a minuscule rump, and the remaining troops were paralyzed and frightened. A sacrifice had to be offered to restore the soldiers' sagging morale by eliciting God's assurances about the outcome of the battle, and Saul, who by now despaired of Samuel's arrival and who was laboring under the pressure of his disintegrating army and the threatening Philistines, initiated the offering without the presence of the prophet. As recounted in the story, the timing of Samuel's arrival seems far from accidental.[6] He arrived at Gilgal almost immediately after the frantic Saul had offered the sacrifice on his own:

> And it happened as he finished offering the burnt offering that, look, Samuel was coming and Saul went out toward him to greet him. And Samuel said, "What have you done?" And Saul said, "For I saw that the troops were slipping away from me and you on your part had not come at the fixed time and the Philistines were assembling at Michmash. And I thought, 'Now the Philistines will come down on me at Gilgal, without my having entreated the LORD's favor.' And I took hold of myself and offered up the burnt offering." (1 Sam 13:10–12)

To Saul's reasonable, distressed, and apologetic account, Samuel offered a rebuke fashioned deliberately to inflict maximum psychological distress:

> And Samuel said to Saul, "You have played the fool! Had you but kept the commandment of the LORD your God that He commanded you, now the LORD would have made your kingdom over Israel unshaken forever. But now, your

kingdom shall not stand. The LORD has already sought out for Himself a man after His own heart and the LORD has appointed him prince to his people, for you have not kept what the LORD commanded you." (1 Sam 13:13–14)

Thus did a venial cultic transgression that could have been excused given Saul's parlous military posture provide Samuel the opening he was apparently seeking to bring Saul down.

Turning worthy ends into dispensable means, including the instrumentalization of religion and the sacred by rivals for power, is a central theme in Samuel, and it surfaces already in this short and harsh encounter. An offering has to be sacrificed before the battle. The king, who in the new dispensation has been divested of any significant religious role, has been made dependent on the comings and goings of the prophet, who had insisted that he must preside personally over the offering. The prophet's claim to an exclusive role in religious ritual became a tool to be used in a competitive struggle manipulated by the personally embittered prophet. Samuel used his presumptive monopoly over ritual sacrifices to shake the throne of the anointed king. Saul had been compelled by a combination of desperate battlefield conditions and Samuel's arrival at the very last minute to disobey the prophet's command. It is difficult to avoid the reasonable speculation that Samuel's resentment and wish that Saul would fail was at the heart of this sequence of events.

After Saul's first stumble as king, orchestrated by Samuel and wrapped in a religious aura, Samuel, who had anointed Saul, now ominously prophesied the end of his reign. Samuel's all-too-human motivation is accentuated in the narrative by an embellishment that the prophet artfully added to his condemnation of Saul's trespass. Samuel claimed that a substitute for Saul had already been picked by God, anticipating a divine decision that the reader knows has not yet been made, in order, as it were, to nail Saul's coffin shut in advance.[7] God's own voice is notably absent from the drama because, at this moment, God and cult have become mere instruments in a struggle between contestants for power. The angry prophet did not accompany the king into battle, and Saul was left alone to prosecute the war: "And Samuel arose and went up from Gilgal on his way, and the rest of the troops went up after Saul toward the fighting force" (1 Sam 13:15). Relinquishing power, including the dynastic power to pass on one's authority to one's male heirs, is difficult even for a religious virtuoso like Samuel. That competitive emotions swirl violently around the winning and losing of hereditary power seems to be the principal lesson of this episode. Samuel used his religious prestige to demoralize and deflate the person he viewed, with very little justification, as his undoer. What the author of Samuel conveys by this striking episode is how religion, even when sincerely believed, can be instrumentalized in power struggles and how political rivals can shed moral qualms about treating the sacred as just another weapon to be opportunistically deployed in a competitive struggle for prestige and power.

Saul's next cultic failure severed the relationship between Saul and Samuel forever, this time accompanied by God's explicit repudiation of Israel's first anointed king. The final fracture occurred after Samuel had commanded Saul, in God's name, to engage in a holy genocidal war of annihilation against the Amalekites. Although he dutifully killed all the Amalekites, Saul saved from the slaughter the best of the cattle and the king of the Amalekites, an act prohibited in a holy war marked by *herem*, which forbade the use of any spoils of war for human purposes.[8] Upon hearing of Saul's transgression, Samuel confronted him, declaring again in harsher terms God's rejection of Saul's kingship. After recording the stinging reproach, the narrator paints a vivid and painful scene of the parting of the ways between the scornful prophet and the devastated monarch:

And Samuel turned round to go, and Saul grasped the skirt of his cloak, and it tore. And Samuel said to him, "The LORD has torn away the kingship of Israel from you this day and given it to your fellowman, who is better than you. And, what's more, Israel's Eternal does not deceive and does not repent, for He is no human to repent." (1 Sam 15:27–29)

The divine rejection of Saul was declared to be eternal, transcending, like God's own word, all human mutability and change. In the last verse of this drama one cannot avoid sensing the bitter irony implicit in the narrator's report that God now rued the coronation of Saul: "And Samuel saw Saul no more till his dying day, for Samuel grieved over Saul, and the LORD had repented making Saul king over Israel" (1 Sam 15:35).[9] God's everlasting commitment turns out to have been contingent and reversible, but only against Saul, not in his favor.[10] Nevertheless, till his last breath Saul will doggedly seek to falsify the prophet's dark prediction. His remaining life struggle and the utter loneliness of the futile quest to retain his hereditary throne will turn him into one of the Bible's most tragic figures.

The poisonous seeds of insecurity and expected loss were now planted ineradicably in Saul's soul. But rather than yielding to the inevitable and relinquishing power after being disowned by God, Saul became completely identified with his royal office. The guileless man who had acceded only reluctantly to the throne now became obsessed with keeping it. The foretelling of his deposition made him cling ever more desperately to power. The maddening cycle of paralyzing self-doubts and frenzied efforts to beat back threats to his power were magnified by Saul's knowledge that his substitute, "who is better than you," had already been chosen and was waiting in the wings. His rival, the one who would end Saul's dynasty even before it passed on to the next generation, was David. And the presence of a challenger, who offered Saul's followers reasons and incentives to abandon him, pushed Saul over the edge. So thoroughly does hereditary sovereignty captivate the one who wields it that the fearful anticipation of losing it, even for one who did not orig-inally seek it, suffices to unhinge the mind.

We first encounter David in the chapter that follows Sam-uel's terminal breach with Saul. Expressing his determination to replace Saul, God ordered Samuel to travel to Bethlehem to Jesse's family and anoint Saul's successor, a command to which Samuel responded with great trepidation: "How can I go? For should Saul hear, he will kill me" (1 Sam 16:2). Saul, who in his youth had to be dragged from hiding in the gear to become king, had now become a murderous threat to anyone, including the prophet, who might put his throne in jeopardy. This is how supreme power can utterly remake the man who is allowed or compelled to wield it.

To protect the prophet from Saul's predictable fury, God sug-gests that Samuel pretend to be going to Bethlehem not to anoint the next king but simply to officiate over a festive ritual sacrifice to which Jesse and his family can be unobtrusively invited. Sam-uel adopts God's alibi and, after fruitlessly considering Jesse's eldest seven sons,[11] has the youngest son David fetched from shepherding the herd and anoints him in the presence of his brothers. "And the spirit of the LORD gripped David from that day onward" (1 Sam 16:13).

Saul's replacement has now been selected, and when he en-ters the scene he naturally appears to be a mortal rival to the sitting king. Our narrator heightens the dramatic and psycho-logical effects of this rivalry by locating David, with virtually no transition, at the court of Saul and indeed in Saul's inner-most circle. In such intimate proximity, a lethal rivalry over supreme political power becomes entangled in a complex web of personal relationships between Saul, his family, and David. The dramatic unfolding of these familial entanglements and confrontations allows the narrator to explore in ever-greater depth how the emergence of a centralized and inheritable sov-ereign authority over all Israel inevitably gave rise to a ruthless and, for Saul, emotionally fraught winner-take-all struggle for power.

The Book of Samuel offers us two distinct accounts of how David, the shepherd from Bethlehem who has been secretly anointed, joined Saul's inner court. According to the first version, Saul, a doomed king holding desperately onto power, sank into a dizzying depression. He had been rejected by the prophet who anointed him and informed that a more talented and lovable rival had been picked to replace him. To relieve the king's chronic melancholy, David was brought to Saul by his servants because of his reputation as a skilled lyre player. David's music had a comforting effect on Saul, exorcising his evil demons, and we are told that "Saul loved him greatly" (1 Sam 16:21). This particular way of introducing David to the court emphasizes Saul's emotional dependency on David. That Saul's mood swings were controlled by David's music foreshadows the way that Saul's emotional life will be defined by his struggle with David. Saul will vacillate uncontrollably between a bitter hatred toward his rival and a loving recognition of him as almost an adopted son.

In the second account of how David joined Saul's court, David was brought into Saul's inner court not through David's soothing musical gifts but due to his heroic and ambitious qualities. According to this account, Saul first became aware of David when David the young shepherd was dispatched by his father to carry supplies to his older brothers, soldiers in Saul's army facing the Philistines in the Elah valley. While the two armies stood confronting one another, Israel's army was challenged by Goliath the Philistine to select a man willing to fight him in single combat to determine the outcome of the battle. Upon hearing Goliath's challenge to Israel and the prize that was promised by the king to the one who would dare fight Goliath, David volunteered to face the giant and was brought before the skeptical king. David's confidence and ambition and the paralysis of the rest of the troops ultimately convinced Saul to allow the young shepherd to fight.[12] After David resoundingly defeated Goliath, he joined Saul's court, becoming one of the king's leading and most trusted officers.

David had a meteoric rise at court. His charisma was irresistible. Saul loved David, Saul's children Jonathan and Michal loved David, and so did all Israel and Judah. In stark contrast to the politically reluctant Saul, David is depicted in the narrative as ambitious and completely at ease on center stage. Over time, the insecure and melancholy king began to perceive David's rising popularity as a threat. As often occurs under the pressure of such emotions, a single incident brought Saul's latent hostility and jealousy to a boil:

> And it happened when they came, when David returned from striking down the Philistine, that the women came out from all the towns of Israel in song and dance, to greet Saul the king with timbrels and jubilation and lutes. And the celebrant women called out and said, "Saul has struck down his thousands and David his tens of thousands!" And Saul was very incensed, and this thing was evil in his eyes, and he said, "To David they have given tens of thousands and to me they have given the thousands. The next thing he'll have is the kingship." And Saul kept a suspicious eye on David from that day hence. (1 Sam 18:6–8)

Saul had not conspired to become king. But now, driven by compulsive suspicion and fear, Saul started plotting to retain the throne, in defiance of Samuel's prophecy, by first covertly and then overtly compassing David's murder. It is in exploring Saul's desperate efforts to maintain the power previously thrust upon him, and thereby dramatizing the psychological grip that supreme political authority exercises over its wielder, that the author of Samuel returns to another one of the deepest and most problematic features of political life—a specific form of self-defeating instrumentalization. In detailing the rise and rule of two very different kings, our author reveals the theoretically fascinating connection between treating ends as means and treating means as ends. As mentioned at the beginning of the chapter, this is arguably one the Book of Samuel's central themes and perhaps the one most resonant with political life as we continue to experience it today.

By refusing to acknowledge moral restrictions on legitimate methods for eliminating rivals who threaten to lure away their military and political supporters, seekers and wielders of sovereign authority end up using the power they have been granted for the welfare of the community for the hollow purpose of clinging to political power for its own sake. This theme emerges with unforgettable force in one of Saul's plots to have David killed. Saul heard that his second daughter, Michal, was in love with David, setting in motion a protracted and complex plot: "And Michal the daughter of Saul loved David, and they told Saul, and the thing was pleasing in his eyes. And Saul thought, 'I shall give her to him, that she may be a snare to him, and that the hand of the Philistines may be against him.'" And Saul commanded his servants:

> "Thus shall you say to David: 'The king has no desire for any bride price except a hundred Philistine foreskins, to take vengeance against the king's enemies.'" And Saul had devised to make David fall by the hand of the Philistines. And Saul's servants told these words to David, and the thing was pleasing in David's eyes, to become son-in-law to the king. And the time was not done, when David arose and went, he and his men, and he struck down among the Philistines two hundred men, and David brought their foreskins and made a full count to the king, to become son-in-law to the king, and Saul gave him Michal his daughter as wife. And Saul saw and marked that the LORD was with David, and Michal the daughter of Saul loved him. And Saul was all the more afraid of David, and Saul became David's constant enemy. (1 Sam 18:21–29)

In the plan that Saul devised, Michal's uncalculating love became bait to lure her beloved to his death. Saul, we are told, was pleased to hear of his daughter's love of David, though he was not happy in a way we would expect a father uninvolved in a lethal contest for power to be. Instead, he connived to use her unscripted love in a plot to eliminate his rival to the throne. The Philistines would savagely resist, he naturally assumed, and David would be the one to die. The narrative emphasizes Michal's intensely vulnerable condition by its unprecedented ascription of love of a woman for a man. As Robert Alter notes, it is the first and only time in biblical literature that a woman is described as loving a man.[13] That his daughter would be devastated if his scheme succeeded didn't enter Saul's calculus in any way. Whatever paternal affection he may have felt for his female child was as nothing compared to his desire to maintain power for himself and his male descendants. He had no qualms about using Michal's wholly noninstrumental love as one more instrument to deploy in his ultimately futile attempt to retain his hereditary crown.

The plot might possibly have succeeded. This is because Saul, who by now understood the workings of ambition and lust for power, was certain that David, too, would not hesitate to use Michal's love as an instrument to serve ends of his own. And this assumption proved correct. Here too, as in the rest of the narrative, David's inner life, as Robert Alter pointed out, is meticulously kept opaque.[14] While detailing how everyone was enamored of David, the narrator avoids mentioning anything about David's own feelings. Jonathan loved him deeply. But did David love Jonathan? Did he love Michal? We don't know. Opaqueness is intrinsic to the mystique of charisma. Screening David's subjective intentions and sentiments from the reader's view is one of the ways in which the genius of our author constructed David's aura. But the general illegibility of David's motives did not prevent Saul from foreseeing that David, too, would have no qualms about using Michal's love as a stepping-stone to power. A royal marriage would presumably enhance his legitimacy in the future. In his dialogue with Saul's servants, David, always the astute tactician, refrained from openly flaunting his eagerness to marry into the royal family. But Saul understood that this apparent reserve had been merely a subtle ploy. They both wished to use Michal, although David aimed to use her to forge a political alliance, while Saul schemed to use her to murder the man she loved.[15] While David's way of treating Michal instrumentally was typical for traditional societies, Saul's way was morally depraved. As it turned out, in any case, David won this round, delivering twofold the requested hundred foreskins and obtaining thereby a legal connection to the king's household that would abet his unspoken ambition to succeed Saul on the throne.

In its essence, love is a noninstrumental relationship. The other whom you love is not solely a means to your end. You care for the beloved person for his or her own sake. Yet Saul's treatment of his daughter as an instrument in a plot to kill her beloved violated the protection that parental love is supposed to grant. Michal's story epitomizes the problem of instrumentalizing essentially noninstrumental relations, since it concerns the way in which the quest for power corrupts its wielders and seekers to the point of debasing love itself. Uninhibited political instrumentalization, our author implies, spreads its poisonous reach into what should be the most secure fabric of human relations—the father's love for his children.[16]

II

In multiple ways, David's character is portrayed as diametrically opposed to Saul's. Without wishing to simplify or flatten the complex portrayals of both, we can say that Saul is generally self-doubting, unambitious, and insecure, while David is generally entitled, ambitious, and self-assured. While Saul is perpetually tormented, prone to panic, and transparent, David is unfalteringly cool, calculating, and opaque. Such a clash of human personalities undoubtedly adds to the quality and richness of the narrative, but more importantly, it provides the author with another perspective from which to explore sovereign power when wielded by political personae with radically different dispositions.

Our emphasis thus far has been on the various ways in which our author explores the double reversal at the core of politics: turning means into ends and ends into means. This double reversal is a central feature of the reigns of both Saul and David. But the Saul/David contrast serves to uncover a third poignant theme, whereby this double reversal, in David's case, results in an irreducible ambiguity of political motivation and political action. A deeper look into the contrast between Israel's first two kings is necessary before we can fully unpack that third theme.

Unlike Saul, David is portrayed as a figure at home with power. He is controlled and confident—a resilient, effective, and charismatic warrior. The sharp differences between the two are already clearly etched by the way each initially steps into the story. David springs into the narrative as a young shepherd who has single-handedly killed both lion and bear while protecting his flock and who has now volunteered in the presence of more experienced yet intimidated warriors to protect the Israelite nation by facing the giant Goliath in single combat. This debut sets him apart from Saul, who first appears as a young man sent by his father to locate some stray asses and who, wholly against his will, was anointed king. It was perhaps this contrast that, among other factors, fueled Saul's jealous rage.[17] Power seemed to come too easily to David; he wore it lightly, without sweating. Saul wished to be like him but was unable to do so. The seeming effortlessness of David's rise was yet another reason why an often-struggling monarch became utterly obsessed with destroying a challenger with whom he could not compete in personal adroitness and charisma.

Saul's flailing efforts to maintain his and his dynasty's claim to the throne, in the face of God's decision to the contrary, led to stark raving madness. One of the essential features of the condition of madness is psychic exposure. A mad person sheds the thin layer that ordinarily masks the chaos of inner life from the outside observer. He walks in the world stripped of the psychological skin with which the "sane" shield themselves. Saul's transparent state of mind was thus an expression of his derangement. His uncontrolled rage precipitated a dissolving of the boundaries of the self. This psychological disintegration is depicted, in a stroke of genius by our author, as an episode of ecstasy: "And on the next day, an evil spirit of God seized Saul and he went into a frenzy within the house when David was playing as he was wont to, and the spear was in Saul's hand. And Saul cast the spear, thinking, 'Let me strike through David into the wall.' And David eluded him twice" (1 Sam 18:10–11). In the Hebrew original, the description of Saul's state of mind "went into frenzy" is conveyed by the verb "va-yitnabe," which literally means "and he prophesied." Prophecy, at times, is a condition of ecstasy in which the boundaries of the self are effaced to give way to the word of God that will overwhelm the prophet.[18] Music, too, sometimes has the effect of dissolving the rigidly bounded self and may therefore lead to ecstasy. But Saul's "prophetic" loss of self occurred despite the music David was playing to soothe him. In that state, resembling ecstatic prophecy, what entered Saul's torn and unshielded self was not God's word but rather a convulsive furor that drove Saul deliriously to attempt to murder David with his own hand.

As already mentioned, obsessional efforts to attain and maintain political power can easily become self-defeating. Among the many self-defeating dimensions of power politics epitomized in the life of the heroes of Samuel, the way in which the unconcealed pursuit of power undermines the very aura of power stands out. In one short and rather peculiar incident, the narrative drives the relationship among loss of self, ecstasy, and exposure to an extreme manifestation. The incident occurs as David takes his first steps as a wanted fugitive seeking refuge. Having been threatened several times at the court of Saul, David realized that he had no chance of surviving in immediate proximity to the king and his loyalists. In his last night at the court, David saved his own life in a hurried escape with the aid of his devoted Michal, and he sought refuge at the home of the prophet Samuel, who had earlier anointed him as the future king:

> And David had fled and gotten away and had come to Samuel at Ramah and told him all that Saul had done to him. And he, and Samuel with him, went and stayed at Naioth. And it was told to Saul, saying, "Look, David is at Naioth in Ramah." And Saul sent messengers to take David, and they saw a band of prophets in ecstasy with Samuel standing poised over them, and the spirit of God came upon Saul's messengers and they, too, went into ecstasy. And they told Saul and he sent other messengers and they, too, went into ecstasy. And Saul still again sent a third set of messengers, and they too, went into ecstasy. And he himself went to Ramah, and he came as far as the great cistern which is in Secu, and he asked and said, "Where are Samuel and David?" And someone said, "Here, at Naioth in Ramah." And he went there, to Naioth in Ramah, and the spirit of God came upon him, too, and he walked along speaking in ecstasy until he came to Naioth in Ramah. And he, too, stripped off his clothes, and he, too, went into ecstasy before Samuel and lay naked all that day and all that night. (1 Sam 19:18–24)

The king of Israel lay naked in an ecstatic state, stripped of his aura, exposed and incapacitated in front of the prophet and the rival he was desperately plotting to destroy. The verb that captures Saul's ecstatic state of mind in this passage—"to prophesy"—is the same verb that was used in the description of Saul's murderous rage. It signifies the unraveling of the self that is shared by both states. The frenzied attempt to hold onto power made Saul internally powerless. Naked and therefore stripped of the regalia of power, his manic breakdown was an outcome of the corrosive effects of this pursuit. Lying naked and dispossessed of all the marks of authority, Saul's personal weakness and emotional breakdown became manifest. That kind of mental collapse, in its extreme forms, is displayed in two ways—in an incapacity to hide one's inner life culminating in the dissolving of the boundaries of the self, and in a radical vacillation of moods and attitudes, caused by a hypersensitivity associated with psychic overexposure and the unraveling of one's personality. The reigning king was afflicted with undefended transparency and vertiginous emotional instability.

III

As Saul is exposed, so David is opaque. David's enigmatic disposition presents another and deeper perspective on the double reversal of means and ends, one that our author explores through the narrative of David's political trajectory from fugitive to king. In David's case, unlike Saul's, the instrumentalization of what should not be instrumentalized is repeatedly suggested without ever being explicitly underscored. David's disciplined and savvy self-restraint open an ambiguous field of action liable to different interpretations, as the voluminous and constantly growing secondary literature shows. But one thing seems clear. David is the master of walking the fine line between innocence and manipulation. The author of the Book of Samuel is less interested in deciding on which side of the line to locate David than in showing what it is to walk that fine line: what it means to defend one's power by exploiting ambiguity, and by fostering a habitual uncertainty in public perceptions of one's underlying character and motivations.

Attempts to unmask David as nothing but a cynical opportunist fail to do justice to the many ambiguities woven artfully into his story. But it would also be naive to locate David wholly on the side of innocence, piety, and saintliness. He was a thoroughly political being operating in a violently competitive environment. Evading Saul's attempts on his life and then going on to seize and maintain royal power were essential to his identity as an immensely shrewd and slippery survivor, not simply the fulfillment of a divinely ordained mission. The author of the Book of Samuel narrates some incidents early in David's political life that reveal his capacity to manipulate the situation to save himself while forcing others to pay the ultimate price. One such incident is described in detail when David, while fleeing Saul's court, still lacked a power base of his own. He arrived alone, unarmed, and with no supplies at the sanctuary of Nob, not far from Saul's court:

> And David came to Nob, to Ahimelech the priest, and Ahimelech trembled to meet David and said to him, "Why are you alone and no one is with you?" And David said to Ahimelech the priest, "The king has charged me with a mission, and said to me, 'Let no one know a thing of the mission on which I send you and with which I charge you.' And the lads I have directed to such and such a place. And now, what do you have at hand, five loaves of bread? Give them to me, or whatever there is." And the priest answered David and said, "I have no common bread at hand, solely consecrated bread, if only the lads have kept themselves from women." And David answered the priest and said to him, "Why, women are taboo to us as in times gone by when I sallied forth, and the lads' gear was consecrated, even if it was a common journey, and how much more so now the gear should be consecrated." And the priest gave him what was consecrated, for there was no bread there except the Bread of the Presence that had been removed from before the LORD to be replaced with warm bread when it was taken away. And there a man of Saul's servants that day was detained before the LORD, and his name was Doeg the

Edomite, chief of the herdsmen who were Saul's. And David
said to Ahimelech, "Don't you have here at hand a spear or a
sword? For neither my sword nor my gear have I taken with
me, for the king's mission was urgent." And the priest said,
"The sword of Goliath the Philistine whom you struck down
in the Valley of the Terebinth, here it is, wrapped in a cloak
behind the ephod. If this you would take for yourself, take it,
for there is none other but it hereabouts." And David said,
"There's none like it. Give it to me." (1 Sam 21:2–10)

Shocked and apprehensive to see David, a high-ranking officer
of the king, traveling alone, Ahimelech was misled by David's
improvised claim to have been sent on an undercover mission by
Saul. By making Ahimelech a partner to an alleged state secret,
David prevented the priest from double-checking the reliability
of his information, since any attempt at verification might well
have constituted a dangerous disclosure. Here our author reveals
another deep truth about political power. The concealed realm
that inevitably accompanies power politics unavoidably allows
and even invites deception, crime, and cunning. By invoking
the excuse of state secrets, nominally subordinate and obedient
political agents can behave in unmonitored and unaccountable
ways, because investigating the sincerity of their claims and
plans could rend the veil of secrecy that is always presumed to
be necessary—because it sometimes really is. Manipulated into
supplying David with food and arms, Ahimelech became an
inadvertent accomplice to a crime, helping an aspiring usurper
escape the punitive hand of the established authorities.

As in many such cases, one lie does not suffice. Pushed by the
circumstances at the sanctuary, David had to add other layers
of deception, this time instrumentalizing not only the priest's
discreet respect for state secrets but the sacred itself. The priest,
we are told, had only consecrated bread at his disposal and
worried about defiling it. David, who needed the whole of the

supply for his escape, fabricated the existence of a group of lads who were waiting for him in another place due to the secrecy of his mission, and he vouched as well for their state of ritual purity. The priest's anxiety was assuaged by the two lies—David is a loyal officer of the king on a clandestine mission, and his entourage is waiting at an undisclosed location in a state of purity. Cozened by these untruths, Ahimelech handed David the consecrated bread.[19]

The sacred is one of the most difficult concepts to grasp. Yet sacredness has a constant and essential feature. Like love, the sacred is essentially noninstrumental. It is the realm that is normatively protected from human manipulation and use. For example, in describing the sacredness of the synagogue structure, the *Mishnah* says that one cannot use its space as a shortcut between two streets; its territory can't be utilized or manipulated for human purposes.[20] The deceptive acquisition of the consecrated bread was therefore another boundary that was transgressed by David, who was driven, by a winner-take-all political competition in which the alternative to victory is death, to embrace without compunction the uninhibited instrumentalization of that which, viewed morally, should never be instrumentalized.

In making the priest complicit in his escape, David put Ahimelech's life at risk, and this maneuver, while arguably saving David's life, proved scandalously fatal for the priest. In the midst of the dialogue between David and the priest, the narrator reveals an important fact that will have a grave impact on the fate of Ahimelech and his family. Doeg, a member of Saul's court who happened at the time to be in the temple, had witnessed the entire affair firsthand. Doeg's testimony to Saul of what occurred at the sanctuary will lead directly to the massacre of the priests of Nob. In the next chapter we will provide a close reading of the section in the narrative that describes the barbarous crime against the innocent priests, but one detail is worth mentioning already here. When Abiathar, the only survivor of that massacre, informed David of the grim fate of the priests at Nob, David admitted that he had been fully aware of the presence of Doeg at the sanctuary and of exactly what it would entail: "And David said to Abiathar, 'I knew on that day that Doeg the Edomite was there, that he would surely tell Saul. I am the one who caused the loss of all the lives of your father's house. Stay with me. Do not fear, for whoever seeks my life seeks your life, so you are under my guard'" (1 Sam 22:22–23). David could have excused his manipulation of Ahimelech by presuming that Doeg would keep quiet, or that in the event that he didn't maintain his silence, Ahimelech would survive by telling Saul that he had been deceived by David. But David already "knew on that day" that neither excuse would hold. With his life and therefore his divinely promised accession to the throne at stake, David naturally refused to tell Ahimelech the truth and give him the option to judge for himself if he wished to assume such risk. Here we return to the Book of Samuel's systematically ambiguous perspective on politics as a sphere of action driven by necessity but suffused with haunting compromises. David made Ahimelech a disposable instrument of his survival at a morally unconscionable and politically typical human cost.

Summoning the courage to confront a giant in single combat may be easier than overcoming an innate sense of entitlement or belief in one's providential mission, however steep the cost to others. In narrating the incident at the temple of Nob, our author established the fact that David, an exemplary seeker of political power, felt no scruples about sending his fellow Israelites to their unjust deaths, although he retrospectively acknowledged their descendants' right to some form of compensation. The way David's motivations and character are shaped by his competitive struggle for sovereign authority is revealed in the early stages of his flight from Saul's court. David's unsqueamish act of throwing Ahimelech and the priests of Nob to the wolves will cast a shadow of doubt over other more ambiguous moments in the narrative to come, enabling our author to develop a deeper phenomenology of political motivation, agency, and self-presentation.

IV

A central moral and political dilemma of the Book of Samuel is rooted in the dynamics of inherited kingship. The logic of dynastic monarchy defines the field of systematic ambiguity in which Samuel's power-seekers and power-wielders necessarily operate and interact. The monopoly of sovereign authority by a single house or lineage not only gives rise to a lethal winner-take-all struggle for supremacy; it also creates, as we now want to show, the fluid line between innocence and manipulation that David skillfully treads. The Book of Samuel contains a story of two dynasties, Saul's and David's, the second replacing the first. In line with the logic of dynastic structures, a usurper of monarchical power cannot permit any members of the previous dynasty to survive. This is a bitter but inescapable rule. If they live, survivors of the ousted dynasty will provide a dangerous rallying point for social forces discontent with the ruling family. Survivors will be resentful troublemakers, constantly conspiring against the upstart family who expropriated their hereditary rights. Any moment of public dissatisfaction with the new king will rekindle their latent hopes for a restoration. It is no wonder that Jonathan, Saul's own son, who loved David and accepted him as the future king, was haunted by the possibility of both his own death and his descendants' extirpation at the hands of David. He even made David swear an oath to alleviate this fear:

> "and the LORD shall be with you [David] as He was with my father [Saul]. Would that while I am still alive you may keep the LORD's faith with me, that I not die, and that you do not cut off your faithfulness from my house for all time . . .

For Jonathan has sealed a pact with the house of David and the LORD shall requite it from the hand of David." (1 Sam 20:13–16)

In the end, David kept only the letter but not the spirit of this sacred oath. Yet David's reputation required its basic violation to be shrouded in ambiguity. Indeed, the detailed account of David's efforts to control his public image, both before and after he becomes king, is a striking feature of the Book of Samuel. It is no exaggeration to say that the principal question raised by our author's tale of two warring dynasties is this: How can David replace Saul without being blamed for regicide and without bloodying his hands with the politically unavoidable extinction of Saul's descendants?

Regicide and the destruction of the former king's family conform to the logic of dynastic monarchy, but raise a religious as well as moral problem: since the king was anointed by a prophet, neither tribal leaders nor the assembled people but God alone should enthrone his replacement. But the transfer of the crown from one family to another poses a dilemma for realpolitik as well. By committing regicide and organizing the extinction of a rival house, the new king runs the risk that he will be widely disparaged as a criminal usurper rather than as a genuinely legitimate monarch. Toppling a ruling dynasty, moreover, sets a dangerous precedent, potentially easing the way for future regicides and bloody depositions. Wielding sovereign authority is dangerous, above all, because supreme power is an irresistible magnet attracting ruthless competition from ambitious and talented rivals to its exercise. Indeed, the essentially contested or fought-over nature of sovereign power is one of the Book of Samuel's basic themes. Gaining such power through violence and murder can easily invite emulation. The very usurper who succeeds in extinguishing the line of the previous monarch risks becoming the next ex-king whose person and family are mercilessly rubbed out.

Saul and his family had to die. But David, aspiring to become not merely Israel's de facto ruler but also its legitimate monarch, made heroic efforts to disassociate himself from regicide and dynasticide. After he acceded to the throne, moreover, he went out of his way to publicize his noninvolvement in the piecemeal obliteration of Saul's descendants and former power base. The most remarkable example of the political deftness with which David dissociated himself from his predecessor's fall from power occurred at the cave in the Judean desert.

David had already been a fugitive for some time, hunted like a wild animal by Saul and his troops. He had gathered some men around him, consisting of his close loyal family and other shady characters who, like David, were fleeing the law. His "army" was but a band of six hundred men skulking along the desert borders of the Judean land in untamed, inaccessible terrain. Apprised of David's location at En-gedi, Saul organized an expedition to reach David and kill him. When Saul's forces approached En-gedi, where David had been reported to be ensconced, David and his men were hiding in the depths of a cave nearby. By chance, Saul entered this very cave to relieve himself, and David's men begged permission to seize the occasion and kill the fortuitously unprotected king, thereby ridding themselves once and for all of their tenacious pursuer.

Refusing to allow such a perfidious stab-in-the-back and indeed holding his men in check, David decided instead to cut off the skirt of Saul's cloak. It was a symbolic act of destruction aimed at the king's vesture, and David made sure to express regret even for this minimally invasive and seemingly impulsive act:

> And it happened then that David was smitten with remorse because he had cut off the skirt of the cloak that was Saul's. And he said to his men, "The LORD forbid me, that I should have done this thing to my master, the LORD's anointed, to reach out my hand against him, for he is the LORD's anointed" (1 Sam 24:6–7).

Being himself one of God's anointed, David carefully instructed his loyalists that the anointed are hedged with divinity and must never be injured in any way. To illustrate David's respect for this political-theological prohibition, Saul was allowed to exit the cave alive. At this point, in a daring move, David followed him into the open, running a risk that might well have cost him his own life and the lives of his men. In order to rebut in advance suspicions that he might conceivably conspire to commit regicide, he shouted out to Saul:

> "My lord, the king!" And Saul looked behind him, and David knelt, his face to the ground, and bowed down. And David said to Saul, "Why should you listen to people's words, saying, 'Look, David seeks to harm you'? Look, this day your eyes have seen that the LORD has given you into my hand in the cave, and they said to kill you, and I had compassion for you and said, 'I will not reach out my hand against my master, for he is the LORD's anointed.' And, my father, see, yes, see the skirt of your cloak in my hand, for when I cut off the skirt of your cloak and did not kill you, mark and see that there was no evil or crime in my hand and I did not offend you, yet you stalk me to take my life. Let the LORD judge between me and you, and the LORD will avenge me of you, but my hand will not be against you. . . . The LORD will be arbiter and judge between me and you, that He may see and plead my case and judge me against you." (1 Sam 24:9–17)

Although he purportedly regretted having cut off the skirt of Saul's cloak at the cave, David put the clipped vestige to an impressive political use, exhibiting to Saul and the onlooking soldiery his innocent intentions, a state of mind that would otherwise have been hidden unobservably within his own conscience and thus impossible to prove to skeptics. By exhibiting the skirt, David demonstrated that Saul's life had been David's to end, and that David had honorably refused.[21] In the event, this outward badge of David's inner innocence, as well as his willingness to

expose his own life to Saul's wrath, also disarmed the vacillat-
ing Saul, whose chronically unstable attitude suddenly flipped
from homicidal rage to heartfelt love: "And it happened when
David had finished speaking these words to Saul, that Saul said,
'Is this your voice, my son, David?' And Saul raised his voice
and wept" (1 Sam 24:17). David's artful display of his own innocent intentions, combined with his warning that God would
punish Saul for trying to kill the anointed successor, brought
Saul to acknowledge momentarily that David would indeed be
the future king, but also led him, conscious as he was of the
ruthless logic of dynastic replacement, to beseech David to let
his descendants live:

> "And so, look, I know that you will surely be king and that
> the kingship of Israel will stay in your hands. And now, swear
> to me by the LORD, that you shall not cut off my seed after
> me and that you shall not blot out my name from my fa-
> ther's house." And David swore to Saul, and Saul went home
> while David and his men went up to the stronghold (1 Sam
> 24:21–23).

One question posed by these verses is the degree to which genuine moral and religious beliefs, including a pious expectation
that God alone will judge and depose Saul, motivated David's
decision to refrain from taking the king's life. An obvious alternative is that his behavior at En-gedi was driven by political expediency. On this account, he conformed to publicly accepted
norms of behavior solely to bolster his own future legitimacy.[22]
To the extent that the double reversal of ends and means dominates the political life of those who aim to seize and hold power,
morality itself becomes a matter of tactics. The tactical dimension of such seemingly moral behavior is stressed by its patently
contrived publicity.

Yet for those engaged in an implacable winner-take-all struggle for dynastic kingship, where the choice comes down to killing
or being killed, the very distinction between the moral and the

instrumental, so important to those of us uninvolved in power politics, may effectively disappear. This is especially likely for an entitled or pre-anointed power-seeker like David, who probably viewed his accession to the throne as a divine calling. Did he view the regicide taboo as a genuine norm to be religiously obeyed or as a hollow slogan to be publicly eulogized and privately ignored? Or were moral and instrumental ways of thinking conjoined in his mind? It is impossible to say. What is clear is that David wanted his personal horror at regicide to be publicly notorious, to be dramatized in a much talked about public spectacle.[23] Needless to say, the public cannot look directly into the hearts and minds of their rulers. Private motivations may or may not diverge significantly from public justifications. Observers can never be totally sure. Moreover, political actions remain irreducibly ambiguous in an objective sense as well. The human mind is a tangled skein and thus the motives of human beings, including those of powerful men, are always mixed. Downplaying both the inscrutability and inherent ambivalence of political motivations is the most common mistake made by the many interpreters who cast the Samuel author as a facile debunker and unmasker. Cynical or "Machiavellian" readings of David's conduct are not wholly implausible, of course. The tendency to treat relationships and moral norms instrumentally in the effort to grab and keep power does cast a shadow of duplicity over all political actions, including the winner-take-all dynastic struggle between David and Saul. Even morally good actions can be performed for exclusively instrumental reasons. Arguably, no genuinely political act can avoid raising suspicions in this regard. But this is far from being our author's last word on the motives of would-be kings.

Both the calculatingly public way in which David distances himself from Saul's fall from power and the fine line between morality and tactics that the psychologically opaque David carefully toes accompany David's career as Saul and his dynasty are gradually annihilated. David was not directly or demonstrably

implicated in Saul's and Jonathan's deaths. Saul's three sons, including Jonathan, were killed in the war against the Philistines
at the mountain of Gilboa. Encircled by enemy troops, Saul
committed suicide by falling on his sword. The messenger who
brought David the news of Israel's defeat and Saul's and Jonathan's deaths, however, committed a fatal mistake. He assumed
that David's palpable interest in eliminating a rival dynasty would
make him willing to gloat publicly about the deaths of its leading
members. He wanted to ingratiate himself with David by bringing news that both Saul and Jonathan had expired in the battle.
In order to magnify his status in David's eyes, the messenger even
claimed that he had personally delivered the final blow to the
dying Saul. So he brought to David Saul's regalia, his diadem
and band. But David, upon hearing what had happened, did not
celebrate.[24] On the contrary, in a consciously public display of
lamentation, he tore his clothes. After interrogating the messenger, who happened to be an Amalekite foreigner, he asked him
rhetorically: "How were you not afraid to reach out your hand to
do violence to the LORD's anointed?" (2 Sam 1:14). And immediately following this harsh rebuke, David ordered the messenger's
execution, thereby memorializing his own noninvolvement in
Saul's death and simultaneously reaffirming that no one can ever
be allowed to touch God's anointed.

David's lament and his execution of the messenger may have
been sincere, genuine, pious, and moral. But David's earlier behavior during the fatal war itself raises nagging although ultimately unanswerable questions about his motivations. For some
time prior to the war, in order to protect himself from Saul, the
fugitive David had adopted the last-resort option: going over to
the enemy's side. Being hunted even in the more remote redoubts
of Judah, David offered his services as the chief of a guerrilla band
to Achish, the Philistine king of Gat, thus obtaining shelter in
a domain beyond Israel's jurisdiction. It took a rather complex
maneuver on David's part to cultivate Achish's trust while avoiding overtly hostile actions against Israel. David's band repeatedly

raided desert tribes at the southern extremes of Philistine's territory while pretending that the spoils they brought from their raids came from attacks on Israel's villages and towns. Having enlisted as a mercenary in the Philistine's army, however, David was presumptively obliged to join the military campaign against Israel, the very campaign that led to the war in which Saul and his sons were killed: "And the Philistines gathered all their camps at Aphek, while Israel was encamped by the spring in Jezreel. And the Philistine overlords were advancing with hundreds and with thousands, and David and his men were advancing at the rear with Achish" (1 Sam 29:1–2). Although he had gained the trust of Achish, David was saved at the last moment from engaging in actual combat against Israel due to the suspicions of other Philistine commanders who demanded that David and his men be removed from the battlefield. They didn't want a former Israelite hero, of dubious loyalty, fighting at their side against his own people. Achish was careful to assure David that he personally trusted him completely and that David was being kept off the battlefield only because of pressure from unduly mistrustful Philistine commanders. Angling to solidify Achish's trust, David protested his removal from the front and was sent back south to engage in his own battles, while the Israelites were defeated by the Philistines at the mountains of Gilboa where Saul and his three sons died. The narrator does not say what David would have done if he had not been granted that last-minute reprieve from the battle. Would he have fought against his people to save his own skin? We are not told, and the silence is deafening.[25] All we know for certain is that, in his dealings with Achish, David is consistently portrayed as a master of masking his intentions.

Although David managed to avoid being involved in the war against Israel, his absence from the war, his playing it safe as a passive bystander while his people and king were defeated, raises obviously disturbing questions.[26] David's sin of omission might possibly have been excused given his ongoing struggle to survive Saul's attempts to have him killed. Yet the narrator, deftly calibrating the scene, left open the possibility that, through his absence from the crucial final battle, David intentionally facilitated Israel's defeat in order to seize the throne without being implicated in the deaths of Saul and his sons. The role played by contrived alibis and plausible deniability in David's long political career is too persistent to be entirely accidental. Yet David's moving lament for Jonathan and Saul is ultimately impossible to disambiguate. His mourning may have been a politically expedient way of covering his distance from the battlefront, after the fact, with a patina of grief. Or, alternatively, it might reflect a genuine sorrow felt, despite his mortal rivalry with Saul, when told of their deaths. Sorrow and expediency may be thoroughly intertwined within David's mind, moreover, so that both could be motivating his response simultaneously. Disentangling such mixed motives is beyond the capacity of outside observers, as our author makes clear. But that is no reason to conclude that David himself, with all the advantages of introspection, would know for certain what drove him to act the way he did. The rich and tangled complexity of David's character, which accompanies all his public and private actions throughout his long career, powerfully resists all simplistic unmasking.

What cannot be denied is that morally unsavory actions necessary to consolidate David's power are performed by others, while he, although benefiting royally from such misdeeds, always manages to maintain an aseptic distance from them. The fate of Saul's legitimate heirs after the deaths of Saul and his sons in battle is the most noteworthy example. To gain a fuller picture of these processes, we need to develop a more detailed account of the events that transpired in the wake of Saul's death.

After the Israelites were defeated by the Philistines on Mount Gilboa, David proceeded immediately to seize the throne of Judah as a stepping-stone to replacing Saul as king of a united Israel, transferring his band to Hebron, the central city of the tribe of Judah. This was politically the proper place to launch a bid to replace Saul, since Judah was David's tribe and served as his power base. Because the rest of Israel's tribes remained residually loyal to the house of Saul, a civil war ensued between David's followers and Saul loyalists. Saul's dynastic stronghold was the tribe of Benjamin, and the Saulide faction was led by Abner, Saul's cousin and the commander of his army. After the battlefield deaths of Saul and three of his sons, Abner enthroned Ish-bosheth, Saul's remaining son, as a kind of a puppet king over Israel. An all-out civil war between rival dynasties ensued. On David's side, the war was led by his three nephews—Joab, Abishai, and Asahel, the sons of David's sister Zeruiah. Joab, the oldest among them, emerged as David's lead henchman and most powerful general. He will play a complex and decisive role in David's future political life.

In one of the skirmishes of the civil war, while Abner's men were beating a retreat, Asahel, the youngest of the Zeruiah brothers, was pursuing Abner on foot. Abner recognized Asahel and pleaded with him to give up the chase, since Abner, being a more experienced warrior, didn't want to kill Asahel, knowing that such an act would entangle him in a risky blood feud with Asahel's brother, Joab. But Asahel persisted in the pursuit, and Abner, who was left with little choice, killed the young man to save himself. Thus did the political rivalry between Judah and Benjamin become a matter of family honor. When Asahel was killed, Joab became morally obliged by the logic of the feud to avenge his brother's blood.

Slowly, David gained an upper hand in the civil war, and his cause was considerably advanced by a rift that opened up inside what remained of Saul's household. Being the strongman at court, Abner took Saul's concubine to himself, an act that symbolically implied entitlement to Saul's power. Ish-bosheth, the weak king of Israel, reproached Abner for appropriating Saul's concubine and thereby signaling his aspiration to the throne. As a result, Abner, resentful at what he considered lack of gratitude for his service to Ish-bosheth, decided to transfer his loyalties to David. Ish-bosheth's personal insult might have sufficed to motivate such a dramatic shift of alliances. But it is more likely that Abner's decision was prompted by his understanding that David was on the verge of prevailing in the civil war and that he needed to ensure his own future by attaching himself to the probable victor. Abner then began persuading the tribe of Benjamin to accept David's kingship, coming to Hebron to seal the bargain that would make David the king over all Israel. After Abner left Hebron, Joab, returning from a military expedition, received the news that such a deal had been brokered and that Abner, having completed the negotiations, was on his way back north. Apparently keen to avenge his brother's killing, Joab was ostensibly angered by the fact that David, rather than arresting Abner for a blood crime against a kinsman, had let him go scot-free. So he sent messengers to bring Abner back to Hebron and, craftily pretending to be his ally in line with the new alliance, Joab caught Abner off guard and took his life.

Joab's killing of Abner provides yet another perspective on the problem of treating instrumentally that which should not be instrumentalized. Revenge in a blood feud is a sacred obligation that, like love, is supposed to be noninstrumental. It is a sacred duty owed to the deceased by his relatives, who are morally responsible for avenging his death. And yet Joab, while killing his brother's killer, was simultaneously and consciously eliminating a potential rival who might have undermined his status at David's court. What makes the story even more complex is that Abner was a palpably ambitious schemer who had betrayed his previous weak sovereign to help raise David to the kingship over all of Israel. This opportunistic shift of loyalty had two possible implications, either of which would have sufficed to motivate Joab's decision to eliminate Abner from the scene. On the one hand, Abner was a proven defector with royal ambitions of his own. On the other hand, if Abner proved sincerely loyal to the new king, he might have gained precedence over Joab as commander of David's military forces.

In the drive to retain great power both the moral obligation to avenge the blood of kinsmen and the unflinching loyalty to the legitimate monarch, like love and the sacred, risk becoming dispensable means in service of political ambition. In the end, we cannot be sure about Joab's motives. The ambiguity cannot be dissolved. Did his public justifications accurately reflect his private motivations? Or did he cynically invoke both a sacred clan obligation and a sacred duty to protect David's throne merely for the sake of personal ambition? Or were his instrumental and moral motives conjoined rather than opposed?

We are told nothing about Abner's own hidden calculations. But Joab's murder of his military rival, compassed immediately after Abner had sealed a treaty with David, must have seemed to Abner's supporters like an unforgiveable act of betrayal. It could conceivably have endangered the fragile alliance that emerged between the tribe of Benjamin and David, which was, in turn, politically essential for David's extending his rule to include all the tribes of Israel. To manage these destabilizing repercussions, David had to take immediate measures to distance himself from the murder of Abner. Such distancing was performed by a public spectacle of mourning and grief over Abner's death:

> And David said to Joab and to all the troops who were with him, "Tear your garments and gird on sackcloth and keen for Abner." And King David was walking behind the bier. And they buried Abner in Hebron. And the king raised his voice and wept over the grave of Abner, and all the people wept . . . And all the people came to give David bread to eat while it was still day, and David swore, saying, "Thus and more may God do to me, if before the sun sets I taste bread or anything at all." And all the people took note and it was good in their eyes, all that the king had done was good in the eyes of the people. And all the people and all Israel knew on that day that it had not been from the king to put to death Abner son of Ner. (2 Sam 3:31–37)

David's genius at neutralizing doubters and rallying public support is on full display in this passage. The degree to which the ruler's legitimacy hinges on his ability to cleanse his public image is the more general insight being conveyed. And yet David's grieving would have been more convincing if justice had been fully done and David had punished Joab for murdering Abner. But punishing Joab was too costly politically for a king who needed Joab's services as his lead henchman.[27] Being aware of the incongruity between the public spectacle of mourning for Abner's death, designed to exonerate David in the eyes of Abner's supporters, and the complete impunity granted to Abner's killer, David offered a feeble apology to his circle: "And the king said to his servants, 'You must know that a commander and a great man has fallen this day in Israel. And I am gentle, and just anointed king, and these sons of Zeruiah are too hard for me. May the LORD pay back the evildoer according to his evil!'" (2 Sam 3:39). David's amply recorded ingenuity and fortitude in coping with hardships makes this protest of helplessness ring hollow. The outwardly pious reliance on God to exact condign punishment was an indirect way of stating that the demonstrably loyal Joab remained indispensable to David's rule and was simply too valuable politically to sacrifice for the sake of justice.

When it helps consolidate rather than undermine the ruler's hold on power, justice is much more likely to be done. Saul's remaining son, Ish-bosheth, had been completely dependent on Abner's capacities and support. Abner's death therefore left him even weaker and more exposed. Eventually betrayed by two assassins, officers from his own army, the politically enfeebled Ish-bosheth was decapitated while sleeping in his bed. Opportunely for David's public image, these assassins committed the very same mistake as the Amalekite messenger who had informed David of Saul's battlefield death. They presented the head of Ish-bosheth to David in a bid to win his favor: "And they [the assassins] brought Ish-bosheth's head to David in Hebron and said to the king, 'Here is the head of Ish-bosheth son of Saul your enemy, who sought your life. The LORD has granted my lord the king vengeance this day against Saul and his seed'" (2 Sam 4:8). David responded with the requisite severity, reminding listeners of his morally upright response when faced with the Amalekite lad's attempt to reap a reward by announcing the battlefield deaths of King Saul and his sons:

> "As the LORD lives, Who saved my life from every strait, he who told me, saying 'Look, Saul is dead,' and thought he was a bearer of good tidings, I seized him and killed him in Ziklag instead of giving him something for his tidings. How much more so when wicked men have killed an innocent man in his house in his bed, and so, will I not requite his blood from you and rid the land of you?" (2 Sam 4:10–11)

To complete this public parade of his immaculately clean conscience, David turned the obviously just execution of the two into a brutal public spectacle: "And David commanded the lads and they killed and chopped off their hands and feet and hung them by the pool in Hebron" (2 Sam 4:12).

The last obstacle to David's total consolidation of power over Israel was now removed. Immediately following the death of Ish-bosheth, David completed a pact with the rest of the tribes. Although the consolidation of David's kingship was wholly dependent on the destruction of Saul's dynasty, David had no provable role in bringing it about. Saul and three of his sons died in the war with the Philistines, Abner was killed by Joab, and Ish-bosheth was assassinated by the two foolishly miscalculating officers. By engaging each time in a highly visible act of mourning, David removed himself, in the public mind, from any connections with such events, even though he had obviously gained everything from them. Joab killed Abner, it should also be said, only after Abner had arranged for Saul's daughter Michal, potential mother of male heirs in the Saulide line, to be returned to David's custody where her childlessness could be assured. The timing suggests that Joab was at least partly motivated by fidelity to David's house. In any case, Joab was not punished for his arguably counterfeit revenge killing. He was not removed from power for murdering one of Israel's great commanders. And one still wonders how David could have stayed on the sidelines in the land of Achish while his sovereign and his people were being slain.

David's veiled and ambivalent attitude toward the fate of Saul's descendants is only gradually and sketchily disclosed in our narrative as David secures his kingdom, sitting safe and sound in his Jerusalem stronghold. After Saul's family had been largely decimated, David issued the following request to locate a survivor from the family: "And David said 'Is there anyone who is still left from the house of Saul, that I may keep faith with him for the sake of Jonathan?'" (2 Samuel 9:1). An old slave of Saul's was sought out as a possible source of intelligence on the matter, and he informed David that Jonathan had a surviving crippled son named Mephibosheth living among Saul's old loyalists. Brought to David's court, Mephibosheth approached the king submissively, terrified at what could happen to him as a living remnant of the former, now-deposed dynasty. But David reassured him, restoring to him Saul's household property that David had presumably confiscated after the destruction of Saul's family. These comforting gestures seem completely sincere and wholehearted. Yet David added to the "favor" bestowed upon Jonathan's son another item that sheds an ambiguous light on David's motivations. Keeping faith, in a formal sense, with the oath he had sworn to Jonathan, David arranged for Mephibosheth to eat at his table at court and to be treated as if he were close kin to David: "And Mephibosheth dwelled in Jerusalem, for at the king's table he would always eat" (2 Sam 9:13). Yet this apparent privilege was also a way to maintain tight control over Mephibosheth, making him a virtual prisoner in David's court, a condition underscored by

Mephibosheth's physical immobility, "lame in both his feet" (2 Sam 9:13). In light of this move, David's initial request, "Is there anyone who is still left from the house of Saul that I may keep faith with him for the sake of Jonathan?" acquires a harsher or at least a more ambiguous edge.[28] It is true that David could have publicly justified his move to keep the last crippled remnant of Saul's dynasty under virtual house arrest by invoking his sacred obligation to honor a promise to Jonathan. But, as we have been arguing, justification and motivation, while conceptually distinct, are not always easy or even possible to unscramble in any particular case.

Neither his subjects nor his courtiers can ever be sure that David is motivated solely by political ambition. The moral norms that he so publicly espouses may, after all, provide genuinely independent reasons for action. This irrepressible ambiguity about the underlying motivations of rulers, in fact, helps explain why their moral excuses are politically effective. If we searched for the most conspicuous example of political ambiguity in the Book of Samuel, David's succinct question—"Is there anyone who is still left from the house of Saul that I may keep faith with him for the sake of Jonathan?"—would shine through. By having him ask this question, our author managed to convey subtly the irreducible ambiguity of David's political motivations, capturing simultaneously his generous desire to reach out and bestow a favor, his fidelity to the letter of a sworn promise, and his determined quest to tighten his complete control over the prior dynasty by bringing its lame sole survivor to sit in perpetual custody at his table.

Throughout the narrative, as we have seen, David is artfully portrayed as a brilliantly elusive character treading the fine line between morality and tactics. In his case, the double reversal of means and ends that haunts the actions of both Saul and David produces a further characteristic feature of sovereign power. In his obstacle-strewn rise to power, David will be constantly tempted to treat instrumentally what from a moral perspective should not be instrumentalized. But our author is careful to avoid any sort of crass debunking. David's real motives are never nakedly revealed.[29] Moreover, the reason why David's intentions remain opaque is itself uncertain. One explanation could be that his intentions are hidden by political craft. Another could be that his motives are genuinely multiple and mixed. These two powerful sources of ambiguous motivation and action remain all-pervasive throughout his rise and reign. That ambiguity is one of the most important reasons why his story speaks so directly to students of political power today.

V

In recounting a remarkable episode that occurred while David was still a fugitive and leading a guerilla band in the Judean desert, the author of the Book of Samuel introduces us to an extraordinarily astute woman who intuitively understands the essential role played by demonstrative morality in the legitimation of David's pursuit of, and eventual accession to, royal power. Roaming desert areas at the time, David and his men are surviving on occasional in-kind payments of wool and meat granted by the owners of lands and flocks in exchange for what passes as protection of sheep and property from marauders and wild beasts. As sometimes happens with extortion rackets, one particularly proud owner refuses to comply with what he sees as an outrageous shakedown, no doubt bridling at the veiled threat wrapped in a speciously polite request. His name was Nabal and his refusal to share his wealth with David and his men was especially haughty and defiant: "Who is David and who is the son of Jesse? These days many are the slaves breaking away from their masters. And shall I take my bread and my water and my meat that I slaughtered for my shearers and give it to men who come from I know not where?" (1 Sam 25:10–11).

Nabal could have justifiably argued that he never asked for the services provided by David's armed band of drifters, that he hadn't heard of David, and that he had therefore no intention of paying for alleged protection services. Yet Nabal's refusal to fork over the requested gifts seethed with class superiority and insolence. The social gulf separating a high-status wealthy landowner from a low-status landless gang leader was brought to the surface in this characteristic tug-of-war over the distribution of agricultural surplus. From Nabal's perspective, David was little more than a runaway slave, a nobody, or, even worse, a conspiring usurper who aimed at upending the social structure and who, in any case, did not deserve to share in a rich man's plenty. The gratuitously insulting way in which Nabal delivered his refusal to make the requested "offering" may have sparked David's fury. Or perhaps David coolly calculated that he needed to make Nabal into a visible exemplar in order to discourage other flock-owners from refusing his protection. On hearing that his request had been arrogantly rebuffed, in any case, David vowed not to leave any male member of Nabal's household alive, the innocent included.

As David and his men were on their way to unleash havoc on Nabal's family and estate, Abigail, Nabal's wife, learned from one of her husband's shepherds of Nabal's insulting ingratitude in refusing to pay for what they testified was David's invaluable protection of their flocks. She also knew that David had already set out to destroy Nabal's estate and family. Supplied with whatever goods she was able to scrape together on short notice, Abigail rushed to preempt the looming massacre by supplying David's followers with the very gifts of bread, cakes, meats, and wine that her husband had refused.

Abigail's encounter with David is one of the most memorable instances of both human savviness and personal persuasion recounted in all of biblical literature. Courageously approaching the bloody-minded band and casting her plea for mercy in the language of piety, Abigail addressed that place in David's self-understanding, of supreme importance to our author, where moral expectation bleeds indistinguishably into political calculation: "And so when the LORD does to my lord [David] all the good that He has spoken about you and He appoints you prince over Israel, this will not be a stumbling and trepidation of the heart to my lord, to have shed blood for no cause" (1 Sam 25:30–31). As Abigail here reconfirms, David has already been tapped to be Israel's future king. He therefore naturally needs to consolidate his reputation as a protector whose demands for supplies and manpower cannot be safely refused. But looking tough does not exhaust the ruler's need to control his public image. Israel's future legitimate king must also carefully distinguish himself from the random chieftain of some desert-crawling protection racket. To legitimate his authority to extract resources from the population, he must do his best to appear not only calculating and ruthless but also lordly, discriminating, and virtuous. He must refrain from blotting his record with unnecessary bloodshed. And above all, as we have already seen, he must keep his personal fingerprints off the violent deaths of personal enemies. In his resolve to punish Nabal's contemptuous refusal to disburse some of his hoarded foodstuffs in exchange for protection, David momentarily lost sight of the essential role played by both demonstrative morality and the inscrutably ambiguous motives of rulers in political calculation. That is to say, he had forgotten the all-importance of plausible deniability in the maintenance of legitimate authority. Abigail's shrewdly crafted speech, delivered with an extravagant self-abasement calculated to flatter a roving bandit seeking to become a sitting monarch, jolted him back to his senses. He therefore thanked her profusely for her sage political advice and ended up taking her as his wife soon after learning of Nabal's sudden death, which came with apparent serendipity as an act of God, untraceable to David's desire for exemplary punishment or revenge. That all the guiltless males in Nabal's house were spared while the guilty Nabal alone died was presumably the moral aim sought and achieved by Abigail's plea.[30] But David's pliant bending to her entreaties brings the irreducible ambiguity of his motives into sharp relief. The extent to which amoral raison d'état alone dictates his acquiescence remains entirely uncertain. Through Abigail's intercession, then, our author sheds crucial light on an essential element of political action. After his temper cools, for David as for all shrewd political players, freedom from petty malice and spite, like the duty to punish the guilty and spare the innocent, is desirable in itself. But it can also be feigned or learned, on realpolitik grounds, in a bid for much-needed political legitimacy.

The stark contrast between the exposed Saul and the elusive and opaque David, dueling for sovereign power, allows our author to convey two deep lessons about the nature of political power and those who seek and possess it. The case of Saul embodies and illustrates a central paradox of political ambition. Whoever chooses to treat love, duty, or the sacred instrumentally for the sake of gaining and maintaining power ends up confined claustrophobically to the airless and companionless prison-house of power, bereft of any humanly worthy life-purpose, focused without respite on retaining power for the mere sake of retaining power. The case of David, by contrast, drives home the inescapable ambiguity of political action. Actions that turn out to have been politically expedient may have been initially undertaken for sincerely moral reasons. And yet it is no easy matter to identify any political action that is both effective and unambiguously moral. We can never be certain, in analyzing political life, that human compassion or a compelling sense of duty is a genuine motive rather than a calculated pretext. This is a second way in which the lust for power can take total control over the one who seeks or wields it. The qualms and misgivings we recurrently feel whenever we encounter thoroughly political actors stem from a genuine perplexity. Because the corrosive reach of instrumentalization engulfs morality itself, we will never be sure what course of action will be taken by those occupying positions of great political power, even if they have a past record of decency and humanity, when their interest in maintaining that power clashes with the morally upright and honorable thing to do.

VI

In order to sharpen our awareness of this dilemma, the author of the Book of Samuel presents us with several contrasting acts of genuine compassion performed by nonpolitical characters operating completely outside the orbit of power.[31] The moving story of the ghostwife of En-dor is just such a case. We come to know the ghostwife of En-dor on the last night of Saul's life, on the eve of his tragic defeat and battlefield suicide. Preparing for war against the Philistines, whose arrayed forces appear dauntingly powerful, Saul already senses his approaching doom:

> And the Philistines gathered and came and camped at Shunem. And Saul gathered all Israel and they camped at Gilboa. And Saul saw the Philistine camp, and he was afraid, and his heart trembled greatly. And Saul inquired of the LORD, and the LORD did not answer him, neither by dreams nor by the Urim nor by prophets. (1 Sam 28:4–6)

Despairing, isolated, and deprived of the comfort of divine direction by any authorized channel, Saul seeks to learn from a legally prohibited occult source what the future holds and how he should behave: "And Saul said to his servants, 'Seek me out a ghostwife, that I may go to her and inquire through her'" (1 Sam 28:7). At the beginning of the story, the narrator had informed the reader that Saul, adhering to the commandments of the law, had banned all necromancers from the land. The prohibition on seeking knowledge from ghosts was not grounded in biblical law's denial of the accuracy and efficacy of such knowledge, however. On the contrary, such knowledge might well be reliable. But the law nevertheless insisted that God and his messengers must be the exclusive transmitters of prophetic knowledge. In his utterly destitute state, therefore, Saul was reverting to a source that he himself had zealously and piously outlawed in the past.

His servants located for him a woman in En-dor not far from Israel's encampment, and a disguised Saul along with two servants stole from the camp at night to glean from her some knowledge of what was to come. When she heard their request to call up dead spirits to help predict the future, the woman, who initially didn't recognize the disguised Saul, informed them of what they should have already known, namely that the king had banned all necromancers from the kingdom on pain of death. Thus, the ghostwife had reason to fear that such a request might be a trap set to catch her violating a royal proscription, thereby exposing her to execution. Saul tried to reassure her by vowing, in God's name, that nothing bad would happen.

Even though he had been rejected by Samuel, the frightened king was still dependent on the prophet who had originally anointed him. He therefore asked the ghostwife of En-dor to summon Samuel from the land of the dead. When Samuel's ghost emerged from the underworld, the ghostwife screamed, suddenly realizing that it was Saul himself who had lodged the request.[32] She then pointedly blamed him for having deceived her when he vowed that no harm would befall her. Assuring her once again that she was perfectly safe, the now-exposed king urged her to proceed.[33] But, Samuel, when he had been successfully summoned up, had no comforting words and no practical advice to offer to the terrified and disoriented king. In death, Samuel resented Saul just as bitterly as he had done while he was still alive. In harsh words, after reiterating God's irreversible rejection of, and enmity to, Saul, he declared with an almost sadistic zeal that Saul and his sons were to die the very next day: "And tomorrow—you and your sons are with me" (1 Sam 28:19).

The now-broken king was left totally speechless to the point of collapsing on the ground, physically debilitated by Samuel's merciless doomsaying as well as by his own failure to have eaten earlier that day. What comes next is the ghostwife's empathetic and kindhearted response to the hopelessly distraught Saul. It is a rare moment of pure compassion devoid of any trace of instrumentalization. Moreover, the ghostwife's compassion is evoked by the very man who had persecuted her and was in his last day among the living, defeated and unable to promise her any future reward:

> And the woman came to Saul and saw that he was very distraught, and she said to him, "Look, your servant has heeded your voice, and I took my life in my hands and heeded your words that you spoke to me. And now, you on your part, pray heed the voice of your servant, and I shall put before you a morsel of bread, and eat, that you may have strength when you go on the way." And he refused and said, "I will not eat." And his servants pressed him, and the woman as well, and he heeded their voice and arose from the ground and sat upon the couch. And the woman had a stall-fed calf in the house. And she hastened and butchered it and took flour and kneaded it and baked it into flat bread, and set it before Saul and before his servants, and they ate, and they arose and went off on that night. (1 Sam 28:21–25)

Saul's last supper was served to him by a socially marginalized woman who was as disconnected from political power as can possibly be imagined. Moved by the shattered king lying inert on her floor, a persecuted sinner proved capable of a pure act of compassion seemingly beyond the moral capacities of the powerful heroes populating the Book of Samuel. The resentful prophet Samuel had only harsh, unforgiving words for Saul on the last night of his life. David and his band were securely hiding in Achish's territory. The only person willing and able to provide Saul with some measure of warmth and care, feeding him from what little she had in her own home, was the woman of En-dor. [34] Her uncalculating compassion is luminous in a narrative replete with moments of questionable piety and political duplicity. The unambiguously noninstrumental nature of her charitable act is the measure of her distance from the equivocal ways of power-seekers and power-wielders. She is a rare moral hero in a world where morality can rarely escape from the cloud of ambiguity that pervades political life.

TWO

Two Faces of Political Violence

In the world portrayed by the Book of Samuel, organized political structures—especially the powers to tax and conscript—originate in violence. They arise initially from the need to establish an adequate collective response to aggressive and acquisitive predation directed at a community by hostile outside forces. Stemming from existential anxiety and the unending search for security, this originally defensive political project, as the author of the Book of Samuel understood it, is inescapably afflicted by the prospect of a self-defeating turnaround: If the sovereign ruler amasses sufficient power to safeguard his people from outside threats, he will also be in a position to redirect that power to torment and abuse his people with sovereign impunity.

Introduced in the book's account of the origin of Israel's monarchy, this core insight is developed and deepened as the author brings into focus the tortured dynamics by which political rulers commonly appropriate power granted for the common benefit and turn it against their subjects and subordinates. The subtlest features of this imperious rechanneling of political violence from foreign threats toward the king's own subjects go far beyond the potentially unfair but in principle acceptable burdens of taxation and conscription against which the prophet Samuel so heatedly warned. These features are explored through two narratives that recount the king's indefensible killing of innocents—first, Saul's massacre of the priests of Nob in 1 Samuel 22 and second, David's murder of his loyal officer Uriah along with the collateral killing of some of Israel's best soldiers in 2 Samuel 11. Read closely, the beautifully crafted stories of these morally unjustifiable slayings, set in diverse contexts and authorized by two very different kings, convey the Samuel author's penetrating grasp of the origins and nature of political crime.

I

Saul's bloody encounter with the priests of Nob takes place during his maddeningly unsuccessful pursuit of David. At this stage, David has managed to elude his pursuers and survive with the aid of Michal's selfless devotion. Jonathan, too, had warned David that his father was determined to destroy him and that he should run for his life. Saul was increasingly exasperated by the failure of his iterated attempts to eliminate his rival who had by now escaped to the eastern borderlands of Judah. The king was equally aware that Jonathan, who loved David and thought he had done no wrong, had helped save David in the face of Saul's instructions to have him killed. Against this backdrop, the narrative opens onto the darkest episode in Saul's tragic political career:

> And Saul heard that David was discovered, and the men who were with him, and Saul was sitting in Gibeah under the tamarisk on the height, his spear in his hand and all his servants poised in attendance upon him. And Saul said to his servants poised in attendance upon him, "Listen, pray, you Benjaminites: the son of Jesse will give every one of you fields and vineyards, he will make every one of you captains of thousands and captains of hundreds, that all of you should have conspired against me and none revealed to me when my son made a pact with the son of Jesse, and none of you

was troubled for my sake to reveal to me that my son has set
up my servant to lie in wait against me as on this very day."[1]
(1 Sam 22:6–8)

To stimulate the veneration or awe that commands obedience,
sovereign power elevates and thus insulates and isolates its
wielder, attenuating any sense of companionship between rulers
and ruled. Indeed, supreme authority can breed a distrust of subordinates so extreme as to verge on paranoia. It is undoubtedly
true that even paranoids have enemies. But the appearance of a
plausible challenger to the throne can make a spiritually isolated
ruler become morbidly suspicious even of his innermost circle
far beyond the bounds of justifiable wariness. Saul is haunted by
a notional conspiracy to dethrone him in which his own tribes-
men from Benjamin are purportedly colluding with David, who
had allegedly promised them wealth and positions of military
command in exchange for betraying their kinsman Saul.[2]

Focused exclusively and obsessively on clinging to the throne,
Saul treats those around him as nothing more than means for
shoring up his power. But such a pervasive and unrelenting instrumentalization of others fatally corrodes ordinary relations
of trust and fidelity. No one who is so thoroughly dominated
by the desperate drive to maintain power at all costs can experience genuine human relations. Because he uses others to retain
power, moreover, Saul naturally reads the behavior of those
around him as equally instrumental, projecting onto them his
own motives and mode of conduct. And his assessment is probably self-fulfilling since they no doubt see that they are being
treated as so many disposable pawns and so will respond in
kind, attempting to use the one who has been using them. Thus,
Saul's inordinate fear of potential betrayal by members of his
innermost circle was both a source and a consequence of the
self-defeating logic of political instrumentalization.

The royal paranoia and obsessive mistrust that we observe
here are also accompanied by outpourings of narcissism and

self-pity. After accusing his close circle of malign conspiracy, Saul—his inner torments laid bare as his throne begins to totter—mournfully cries that none of his servants or subordinates takes his side or cares for him sincerely. They do not feel his pain. If they haven't betrayed him yet, their defection is only a matter of time. Imagining himself surrounded on all sides by secret or future traitors, he feels utterly forsaken and forlorn.[3] The wounded narcissism on display here segues seamlessly into Saul's piercing sense of victimhood and endangerment. Though he is the one who has been pursuing David with homicidal intent, Saul declares that David, with the complicity of Saul's own son, is lying in ambush to pounce upon Israel's king and take away his life. A well-armed aggressor with considerable forces at his command and who has openly attempted on several occasions to slay David with his own hand, Saul presents himself as a helpless, friendless, isolated victim. Holding the deadly spear with which he had twice tried to pin David to the wall,[4] the wretched Saul—haunted by the thought of conspiracies against him and pleading pathetically for human empathy from the very circle of servants he intensely mistrusts—describes David, the persecuted fugitive, as the real aggressor, furtively plotting regicide. Such an inversion of roles, whereby an emotionally aroused perpetrator describes himself as the beleaguered victim, is frequently a prelude to violence.

Saul bemoans the conspiratorial silence that he feels all around him. Nobody informed him of the secret pact that his son had struck with David. No one can be trusted. So how can political loyalty be convincingly manifested to such a distrustful king? Only by breaking the silence, and that means by providing incriminating testimony to a ruler primed to espy traitors lurking everywhere in his midst. This is what happens next:

> And Doeg the Edomite, who was poised in attendance with Saul's servants, spoke out and said, "I saw the son of Jesse coming to Nob to Ahimelech the son of Ahitub. And he

inquired of the LORD, and provisions he gave him, and the sword of Goliath the Philistine he gave him" (1 Sam 22:9–10).

Saul's plea for a show of loyalty is here answered by an informer, who happens to be a foreign mercenary and Saul's chief herdsman. The information he provides is particularly effective and tantalizing because it plays into Saul's obsession with dark conspiracies. Yet the attending servant Doeg, while indulging the king's paranoia, also skillfully redefines the circle of suspected conspirators. He deflects the king's suspicion from the courtiers in Saul's immediate entourage to a more distant target—Ahimelech, the priest of Nob.

Eager not only to appease and entice the king but also, importantly, to deflect his wrath, Doeg prevaricates. His report severely misrepresents the support that Ahimelech provided to David. Given the previous chapter's detailed account of how David deceived Ahimelech, the reader knows that Doeg's testimony is maliciously false. Having escaped empty-handed to the sanctuary at Nob, as that chapter recounts, David pretended that Saul had sent him on a secret mission. Under these false pretenses, he asked Ahimelech to supply him with food and arms. Misled in this way, Ahimelech innocently complied, handing David the consecrated bread as well as Goliath's sword. But David did not ask the priest to query the word of God for him. Contrary to Doeg's report, Ahimelech did not provide David with any oracular service.

Doeg dishonestly claims that Ahimelech inquired of God at David's behest for two reasons. If Ahimelech had in fact given oracular advice, he would have been acting as David's priest. In that case, Ahimelech would not have been merely helping a royal official in need; he would rather have been subordinating himself to David. A priest ordinarily provides an occult way of communicating with God only to the king who requests it in the direst of circumstances.[5] Doing this for David would have been tantamount to encroaching on Saul's still-sovereign authority.

Another and perhaps more important reason why Doeg misreports David's interaction with Ahimelech at Nob is to lend spurious credence to Ahimelech's personal complicity in an alleged conspiracy against Saul. If David had indeed asked Ahimelech for divine guidance concerning what he should do next, Ahimelech would have been fully apprised of David's status as a fugitive escaping from the king. Moreover, whatever question David would have instructed Ahimelech to pose to God would have surely disclosed David's illicit aims. If Ahimelech had actually inquired of God on David's behalf, as Doeg alleged, Ahimelech could not plausibly plead ignorance of David's treasonous aims.

His hyper-suspicious mind now fully made up, Saul immediately summons Ahimelech and charges him with conspiracy. Doeg's ploy for channeling Saul's paranoia-enflamed hunt for disloyal subordinates away from the king's immediate entourage and toward a distant target has proved brilliantly successful:

> And the king sent to summon Ahimelech the son of Ahitub and all his father's household, the priests who were in Nob, and they all came to the king. And Saul said, "Listen, pray, son of Ahitub." And he said, "Here I am, my lord." And Saul said, "Why did you conspire against me, you and the son of Jesse, giving him bread and sword and inquiring of God for him, so that he set up to lie in wait against me on this very day?" And Ahimelech answered the king and said, "And who of all your servants is like David, loyal and the king's son-in-law and captain of your palace guard and honored in your house? Did I this day for the first time inquire for him of God? Far be it from me! Let not the king impute anything to his servant or to all my father's house, for your servant knew nothing of all this, neither great nor small." (1 Sam 22:11–15)

The lethal mixture of paranoia, self-pity, and rage in Saul's mind has the perverse effect of enlarging even further the range of suspected conspirators. Although Doeg, in his false report to Saul, incriminated only Ahimelech, the perceptive narrator tells us that Saul summoned not only Ahimelech but also his entire household.[6] In his feverishly distrustful mental state, Saul may have reasoned as follows: Ahimelech could not have done it alone; all his kin, everyone close to him, must have been involved. Though Saul addressed Ahimelech directly, his charge in the Hebrew text was formulated in the plural; "Why did [all of] you conspire against me?" As we learn later in the story, Ahimelech's household consisted of eighty-seven men. These wholly innocent individuals were added to the list of the accused conspirators due to a combination of Doeg's conniving mendacity and Saul's unhinged paranoia. In his treatment of political paranoia our author uncovered two of its essential and exceptionally dangerous features. First, as a delusional phobia of being persecuted and conspired against, paranoia is untethered from the reality of any specific enemy or determinate threat. As a result, it can be easily deflected and inflated by courtiers with agendas of their own, illustrating how rulers can be cunningly manipulated by their subordinates. Second, when it feeds on a ruler's deep psychological insecurity, the paranoid fear of the defection of close collaborators has an insatiable quality. Nothing that anyone says or does can put it to rest.

Presenting himself loyally and obediently before Saul as he had been commanded to do, Ahimelech attempted to defend himself from the gravest of Saul's charges. He knew nothing of any conspiracy, he protested. David, the king's son-in-law, was in his eyes the most loyal and respected of Saul's servants.[7] And Ahimelech flatly denied giving David oracular advice or indeed any service that would have made him an accomplice to a treasonous conspiracy.[8] What makes his defense particularly poignant, however, is the way Ahimelech scrupulously refrains from giving a fully exculpatory account of how events actually unfolded at the sanctuary. Given the events reported in the prior chapter, Ahimelech could have easily and accurately added: "I even asked David why he was alone, and he told me that he was sent by the king on a secret mission. David deceived me. I was his dupe not his accomplice. I had nothing to do with the whole thing." So why did Ahimelech, aware that he was facing capital punishment, not inform Saul that he had been taken in by David's trickery?

Perhaps Ahimelech decided not to mention the deception because, paradoxically, bringing it up would have raised the thought that he had, from the beginning, entertained a vague suspicion of David's wrongdoing. He had, after all, trembled noticeably when he saw one of Saul's high-ranking commanders traveling alone. If he had felt that something was amiss, he should have done what he conspicuously failed to do, that is, immediately reported the incident to Saul's court. This explanation of Ahimelech's silence about David's alibi is not entirely implausible. What seems more likely, however, although the thought remains speculative, is that by failing to report David's false claim to have been on a clandestine mission for the king, the priest was motivated by an honorable desire not to incriminate David further. Perhaps he did not want to disclose the latter's willingness to deceive even men of God in his flight from Saul's deadly pursuit.

In the telegraphically brief dialogue between Saul and Ahimelech, in any case, our author highlights the morally significant differences between Doeg, Saul, and Ahimelech. The cunning Doeg deflected the charge of conspiracy from Saul's courtiers to Ahimelech; the paranoid Saul extended this charge to everyone in Ahimelech's household; and the innocent priest not only refrained from channeling any guilt onto David but even strove to protect David while putting in jeopardy his own life.

In the event, Ahimelech's redacted self-defense fell on deaf ears. Saul immediately ordered the execution of all the priests:

> And the king said, "You are doomed to die, Ahimelech, you and all your father's house!" And the king said to the runners poised in attendance on him, "Turn round and put to death the priests of the LORD, for their hand, too, is with David, for

they knew he was fleeing and did not reveal it to me! And the
king's servants did not want to reach out their hand to stab
the priests of the LORD" (1 Sam 22:16–17).

The king's bodyguards balked at his initial order to execute the
priests of Nob. The taboo against killing priests was evidently
one they were unwilling to violate.[9] Their decision to disobey
might have been bolstered by their realization that the charges
were baseless and that the circle of alleged conspirators against
Saul had been unfairly and perversely extended to include all
the priests of Nob. Here our author discloses another important
insight into the dynamics of political violence. Like any sovereign, a king depends on cooperation. His ability to enforce his
commands hinges to some extent on their legitimacy in the eyes
of his armed enforcers. Thus, when those with direct physical
control of the means of violence collectively refuse to cooperate,
his solemnly pronounced commands ring hollow.[10] Saul is a relatively weak king with waning authority. But no ruler, no matter
how strong, can rely solely on coercion to dictate the behavior
of those who wield the means of state coercion on his behalf.
When ordering violence against his own subjects, therefore, a
sovereign is necessarily constrained by the likely unwillingness
of his security forces to obey any order to massacre kinsmen,
their own flesh and blood, who, in this case, were also men of
God.

Saul's way around the defiant refusal of his Israelite bodyguards to carry out his death sentence against the priests of
Nob is typical of autocratic rulers even today. He summoned a
foreigner, a mercenary who shared no bonds of solidarity with
the priests, who had no local power base of his own, and who
therefore depended wholly on the king for his status at court:

And the king said to Doeg, "You, then, turn round and stab
the priests," and Doeg the Edomite turned round and he it
was who stabbed the priests and he put to death on that day

eighty-five men who wore the linen ephod. And he struck
down Nob the priests' town with the edge of the sword, man
and woman, infant and suckling, ox and donkey and sheep,
all by the edge of the sword (1 Sam 22:18–19).

Unconstrained by bonds of blood and kinship, Doeg the Edomite
felt no compunctions about carrying out the massacre. He followed Saul's orders unquestioningly, even though they extended
far beyond his own false testimony, which had implicated only
Ahimelech. He dutifully murdered eighty-seven priests who were
entirely guiltless of the crime with which they were charged. This
brings us to the final insight into the nature of political violence
woven into this episode of Saul's faltering reign.

When the line of justice is breached and capital charges are
lodged against manifestly innocent people, the bloodshed will
not stop at the circle of those initially indicted. No boundary
is set to define and delimit the punishment meted out when ac-
cusations and suspicions are manifestly groundless. The frenzy
of killing, in this case, included every living being associated
with Nob, the young and the infants and even all the domestic
animals. Precisely because Doeg was a foreigner, free from the
constraints of kinship, he also had a pressing need to prove
his loyalty to the king. And there is nothing that demonstrates
loyalty more effectively than willingness to commit a heinous
crime. Carrying out a royal order to slaughter the innocent has
a deeper and darker capacity to bind subordinates to superiors
than the mere bestowing or receiving of a benefit. The tribal
bond of blood that did not exist between Saul and Doeg was
replaced by another bond—a bond of blood guilt that ties ac-
complices together in the wicked and deranged exercise of sovereign power.

Some commentators argue that the massacre of the priests
of Nob was a perfectly rational way for Saul to signal his absolute intolerance for any community throughout the lands of Israel who dared offer sanctuary or nourishment to the fugitive

David. The obvious innocence of the priests of Nob would have made such a threatening message more effective still. But even though such a reading is possible and in some ways appealing, it fails to do justice to our author's persistent stress on the deeply emotional nature of conflict over supreme power. At this point in the story, Saul is presented not as calculatingly rational but as painfully jealous, chronically suspicious, and mentally unbalanced. After repeatedly failing to kill David, Saul's towering rage against David and what David represents seems the most likely motive for Saul's criminal act of indiscriminate overkill.

In our view, the subtly constructed details of the story of the massacre of the priests of Nob reveal how the anonymous author of the Book of Samuel excavates the deepest underpinnings of political violence, uncovering structural themes that emerge when a sovereign turns his capacity for violence, originally bestowed to fend off foreign threats, against his own subjects and subordinates. The Israelite people had knowingly accepted the burdens of taxation and conscription as the price of collective self-defense. But they had not agreed to the massacre of innocent members of their own community, for no legitimate national purpose, by a mentally unhinged and paranoid king.

At the center of the author's analysis of this historically perennial dynamic stands not the cold-eyed use of an indiscriminate massacre to send a warning signal, but rather a deep link between violence and paranoia, between the slaughter of innocents and the all-corrosive distrust fostered by the supreme ruler's disorienting isolation. Power becomes especially dangerous when, as in Saul's case, its wielder turns acutely insecure.

Here we encounter another of our author's penetrating insights into the workings of the human political realm. Competition over supreme power can easily draw the incumbent ruler into a vicious circle. Made insanely jealous and insecure by the sudden appearance of a popular and talented rival to the throne, he will desperately use those around him to maintain his grip on power. But his insecurity, far from being assuaged, will be thereby reinforced. Manipulating everyone in sight leads the sovereign to distrust those around him, since he will naturally project his own scheming and manipulative style onto his courtiers and retainers. This is how deranged defensiveness can breed and heighten emotional insecurity among wielders of great power. Because its object is unspecified, moreover, political paranoia can easily be manipulated, redirected, and extended by royal agents with agendas of their own. The paranoid ruler, sniffing betrayal everywhere, loses control of himself. Far from reflecting a cool calculation of likely consequences, his conduct spirals erratically out of control in response to inconclusive hints of disloyalty, like a leaf tossed randomly about in the wind.

Paranoia wreaks havoc. It strews devastation because of its fluid malleability, vulnerability to manipulation, and tendency to uncontrolled expansion. The great power in the hands of a paranoid king changes the incentives of his entourage, leading them to shade the truth in his presence and choking off even more completely his limited access to reliable information. And his empowered paranoia becomes more lethal still when accompanied, as it often is, by a mentally unhinged reversal of roles, whereby the undoubted aggressor begins, with melodramatic self-pity, to cast himself as the only genuine victim.

When the sovereign's violence is turned upon his subjects for the sovereign's own imagined good, it may meet the resistance of armed subordinates, since those who personally wield the means of violence are often reluctant to use deadly force for an unjust cause against kith and kin. This is why foreigners in the service of power, unhampered by ties of kinship but also feeling a greater need to signal their loyalty in a credible way, are often the ones most willing and able to execute the sovereign's publicly unjustifiable violence upon his guiltless subjects. The sovereign will have to take the risk that his own armed retainers, having resisted his order themselves, will silently acquiesce when the crime is committed by a foreigner, so long as they themselves are not called upon to perform the crime. The morally dubious distinction between action and omission proves very useful for constructing plausible excuses when stakes are high. Passive compliance by those who would never bloody their own hands, our author implies, can be reliably counted on by rulers plotting political crimes.

In our second story, the murder of Uriah by David, the author of the Book of Samuel explores political violence in a different context and under a radically different ruler. In this second account of a king who brazenly sends his own innocent subordinates and subjects to die, our author focuses on a second and distinct facet of political violence, this time involving the question of agency and the obfuscation of political responsibility. We now turn to this second source or form of political crime, one grounded not in paranoia but rather in its opposites: overconfidence, a sense of entitlement, and decadence. As with the massacre of the priests of Nob, honing in on the details of the complex story of Uriah's murder will help us uncover the most significant and consequential themes that emerge from its brilliant construction.

II

David was at the height of his power when he murdered Uriah. He had conquered Jerusalem and, by relocating his court from Hebron—a city at the heart of the Judean lands—to Jerusalem, on the border between Judah and Benjamin, he had risen from the status of a tribal leader to consolidate his kingship over all of Israel. Military success followed. He defeated the Philistines in the west, he subjugated the Edomites in the south, and emerged victorious in his battles over the Moabites in the east. By the time his conquests reached as far north as the Aramean kingdom of Zobah, the narrative portrays David as having risen to the status of a regional overlord. With the help of Hiram, King of Tyre, who sent craftsmen and cedar trees to Jerusalem, a royal palace was built and was now inhabited by David's wives, concubines, sons, and daughters. The only thing missing to complete David's glory was a splendid temple of God, annexed to his palace, which the now-triumphant king also aspired to build. Having promised David an everlasting dynasty, God may have nevertheless hesitated to add this crowning achievement to the king's worldly grandeur. In any case, God refused David permission to build his temple. This symbol of the full consolidation of the Davidic monarchy would have to await the accession of his son and heir.

At the time of his most memorable crime, David's army was engaged in a war against the Ammonites across the Jordan River to the east of Jerusalem. The narrative opens with the following richly revealing scene:

> And it happened at the turn of the year, at the time the kings sally forth, that David sent out Joab and his servants with him and all Israel, and they ravaged the Ammonites and besieged Rabbah. And David was sitting in Jerusalem. (2 Sam 11:1)

This introductory scene, which sets the stage for the crime about to be committed, is artfully sketched. It points to the disturbing combination of supreme self-assurance and decadent self-indulgence in the king's demeanor. His authority over his armed followers was now so secure that he could control the battlefield from the comforts of his palatial home, a point never reached by the weak King Saul. David issued commands from his stronghold in the certainty that he would be obeyed by his trusted and obedient officers at the front. He was no longer a roving bandit or a field commander marching around the rugged countryside alongside his troops. He had become a comfortably stationary king. He evidently felt no anxiety about the ongoing war, and no need to micromanage the way it was being fought.

But the gap between the idleness of the king, "sitting" at home, and his forces arrayed in the open field, engaged in combat, points not only to the consolidation of the Israelite monarchy and David's inveterate self-assurance. It also suggests his self-indulgence, aloofness, and dissipation. We might have excused the absence from the front of a king who, until recently, had been personally leading his troops into combat[11] if there had been an urgent crisis at home that he was obliged to handle in person while eagerly awaiting news from the field. But the subsequent depiction of the king's leisurely routine while his army was waging war at Rabbah eliminates the possibility of such a reassuring explanation:

> And it happened at the eventide that David arose from his bed and walked about on the roof of the king's house and he saw from the roof a woman bathing, and the woman was very beautiful (2 Sam 11:2).

After a prolonged siesta that stretched into the late afternoon, David awoke and wandered on his roof to enjoy the sweet breeze of a Jerusalem evening. He was not preoccupied with the urgent domestic needs of the kingdom. Instead, the serenely self-confident king is portrayed as luxuriating in an easy decadence. Such a state of mind reflects and reinforces a perilous sense of entitlement. He suddenly spots an alluringly beautiful woman from his commanding vantage point on his palace roof, and he reaches out to her through government servants at his beck and call. The unembellished abruptness and staccato pace of what follows convey a powerful sense of a king's irresistible supremacy over his subjects:

> And David sent messengers and fetched her and she came to him and he lay with her, she having just cleansed herself of her impurity, and she returned to her house. And the woman became pregnant and sent and told David and said, "I am pregnant." And David sent to Joab: "Send me Uriah the Hittite." And Joab sent Uriah the Hittite to David (2 Sam 11:3–6).

Unlike the paranoid Saul, who feverishly mistrusted his inner circle, David was coolly confident to the point of recklessness. He felt no particular need for discretion. He sent one messenger to inquire about the beautiful woman and he sent others to fetch her and bring her to his palace. But David's nonchalance conveys more than the careless mind-set of a domestically unchallenged ruler. As other readers of these verses have noted, the verb "send" dominates the narrative.[12] By repeatedly employing this verb, the author wishes to stress a central feature of both the way power is constituted and how it operates.

Hierarchically organized power is defined by the power-wielder's capacity to act from a distance. Delegation involves the capacity to create extended causal chains, embroiling and implicating multiple subordinates whose actions radiate downward from an apex or outward from a center. The longer the chain, the greater the power of the sovereign who acts invisibly through its multiple links. It is as if the arm of the sovereign literally reached its remote objective through a succession of proxies carrying out his commands. So the repetition of the verb "send," which pervades the entire narrative, emphasizes the centrality of acting from a distance to the exercise of great political power. The ruler's numerous messengers, surrogates, and agents serve not only as tools of his power but, more significantly in the present context, as decoys obscuring the initiator's identity and disguising his stage-management of the way the action unfolds.

The power-wielder's remoteness from the field of action is already implied in the opening scene of the narrative.[13] Even before committing adultery and murder, the king luxuriates in Jerusalem while his army is fighting fiercely in Rabbath-Ammon. Admittedly, action-at-a-distance is characteristic of all hierarchical organizations, including the consolidated monarchy of Israel that had now replaced the divinely inspired anarchy described in the Book of Judges. But the genius of the narrative here consists in the way it slowly reveals how, in David's case, action-at-distance, first introduced to depict his conduct of the war from his palace, can also facilitate and encourage political crime. This is because political action-at-a-distance makes public deniability all too easy to convincingly maintain. The creation of a lengthy causal chain and the distribution of tasks among its agents provide a way of artificially dissociating the sovereign from the violence committed on his behalf. This is the dark side of delegation. Action through unacknowledged proxies enables an almost effortless shifting or ducking of responsibility, making it nearly impossible to trace malignly criminal acts to the ruler at whose behest they are committed. The perennial lament, "If only the ruler knew what his agents were doing!" implicitly reflects the ease with which the sovereign's involvement in morally repugnant conduct can be obscured.

After beginning unhurriedly with David's rooftop stroll, far from the cares of war, the narrative speeds up frantically when a chance event suddenly plunges the monarchy into a dangerous political crisis. Uriah's wife, Bathsheba, is pregnant with David's child. It is left uncertain whether the pregnancy was just the accidental result of a momentary infatuation or was instead something Bathsheba may have planned ahead of time. Facing the disastrous consequences of impregnating another man's wife, an ordinary individual might feel overwhelmed with regret or even decide to repent. But sovereign authority is no ordinary tool of human desire. On the contrary, supreme political power is a capacity that radically reshapes motivations and dispositions, an instrument that balloons, even to the point of criminalization, its wielder's purposes and goals. The Uriah episode, universally recognized as a pivotal moment in the David story, allows our author to explore in unforgettable detail an easily overlooked way in which political authority possesses and remakes the ruler who presumably believes he is acting on his own sovereign and unimpeded will. Far from being chosen independently of available means, ends-in-view are inevitably aggrandized by swollen means. Sometimes, at least, wielders of great power do what they do simply because they can. This may seem a trivial point, but it isn't. Rather than rulers wielding political power, it implies, political power wields rulers, toying with their motivations, aspirations, and inhibitions. Sinners with the instruments of sovereign power at their disposal, for instance, rather than feeling pangs of remorse, are irresistibly tempted to "fix" things.

As the narrative vividly illustrates, the omnipotence fantasies inevitably nurtured by the obsequious deference that royal power inspires can quickly draw the wielder of sovereign authority deeper and deeper into the abyss of criminality. Uriah's absence from Jerusalem while performing his duties to the king at the front made it possible for the king to snap his fingers and bed Uriah's lawful wife. The fact that Uriah's personally dangerous service to king and community made David's adultery possible aggravates our sense of the painful gap between the licentious king dallying in his palace and his soldiers risking life and limb at the front.

The king's supreme authority, in any case, means that Uriah can be summarily recalled to Jerusalem from the war. If Uriah will sleep with Bathsheba, David's adultery will be covered up, because the accidental pregnancy will then be publicly attributed to Bathsheba's lawful husband. To establish this alibi, David dispatches a messenger to Joab to summon Uriah to Jerusalem:

> And Uriah came to him, and David asked how Joab fared and how the troops fared and how the fighting fared. And David said to Uriah, "Go down to your house and bathe your feet." And Uriah went out from the king's house and the king's provisions came out after him. And Uriah lay at the entrance to the king's house with all the servants of his master, and he went not down to his house. And they told David, saying, "Uriah did not go down to his house." And David said to Uriah, "Look, you have come from a journey. Why have you not gone down to your house?" And Uriah said to David, "The Ark and Israel and Judah are sitting in huts, and my master Joab and my master's servants are encamped in the

open field, and shall I then come to my house to eat and to drink and to lie with my wife? By your life, by your very life, I will not do this thing." And David said to Uriah, "Stay here today as well, and tomorrow I shall send you off." And Uriah stayed in Jerusalem that day and the next. And David called him, and he ate before him and drank, and David made him drunk. And he went out in the evening to lie in the place where he lay with the servants of his master, but to his house he did not go down. (2 Sam 11:7–14)

In order to dispel Uriah's possible suspicions about why his king had called him back to Jerusalem from the front, David asks him to report on the course of the war.[14] Capable commanders often randomly seek information from ordinary soldiers in order to gain a fresh perspective outside of official channels and independently of the formal reports they regularly receive. Rather than sending Uriah immediately back to the front after hearing his account of the war, Israel's seemingly generous and considerate king then suggests to Uriah that he go home, which we know to be near the palace, assuming that a homesick soldier would not pass up an opportunity so close at hand. But Uriah, always the loyal soldier, insists on maintaining his solidarity with the troops and, rather than enjoying the comforts of home, sleeps near the king's servants at the gate.[15]

As others have noted, Uriah's unwavering refusal to sleep at home might also imply a tacit rebuke of David's own behavior. In his detailed response to the king's urgings that he take advantage of his leave from the front to spend some time at home, Uriah justifies his own self-denying choice by recalling that the Ark, Joab, and all of Israel remain in the open field, unsheltered and exposed to enemy attacks. This renunciation of domestic pleasures when fellow soldiers remain under fire throws into sharp relief the self-centeredness of the king's behavior by contrasting it with the honorable and solidary conduct of everyone else, including the Ark, God's symbolic presence at the front.

David's pleasure-seeking decadence was certainly not going to serve Uriah as a model for the proper conduct of a soldier in wartime. Moreover, by adding to his refusal to go home the detail "to lie with my wife," which was a private matter that the king himself had not explicitly mentioned, Uriah may be hinting that he harbors suspicions about the king's machinations, suspicions that might have been triggered by the king's excessive interest in the whereabouts of Uriah during the night.[16]

We know of course that David had not been especially discreet. Servants were sent scurrying back and forth between David and Bathsheba. Rumors might have circulated around the palace. Sleeping at night among the servants might also be a good way to pick up information about shadowy palace intrigues and goings-on.

Frustrated by the failure of his repeated attempts to conceal his scandalous conduct, David now resorts to a far more brutal method of extracting himself from the dangerous predicament in which his sexual escapade had entangled him. Because Uriah had stubbornly refused to play his assigned role in the cover-up that David had so cagily planned, another and grislier crime had to be committed:

> And it happened in the morning that David wrote a letter to Joab and sent it by the hand of Uriah. And he wrote in the letter, saying, "Put Uriah in the face of the fiercest battling and draw back, so that he will be struck down and die." (2 Sam 11:15)

The letter that David sent to Joab was carried by Uriah himself, who thereby became a messenger delivering his own death warrant. Knowing that Uriah was a fiercely loyal soldier, David trusted him implicitly not to open the sealed letter.[17] And the way David formulates his command allows the author of Samuel to disclose yet another cardinal truth about political violence.

David was able to distance himself from the murder plot he had concocted by orchestrating the circumstances of its execution so that, in the end, it would be the enemy, the Ammonites, who kill Uriah.[18] The burden of committing an act of political violence is thus distributed piecemeal, along a chain of agents. Without the new capacity for action-at-a-distance inherent in hierarchically organized authority, David would presumably never have undertaken, or even imagined, such a heinous crime. The king has the power to command Joab to command his troops, including Uriah, to locate themselves in the forefront of the hottest battle, and then to command the troops suddenly to withdraw, abandoning Uriah to be killed by the enemy.

Effecting outcomes at a distance is the mark of great power, whether employed for morally justifiable or rankly wicked ends. But unjust and unjustifiable killing-at-a-distance becomes perversely and perhaps irresistibly tempting for wielders of such power because the unobservable relation between initiation and execution enables obfuscation of agency and evasion of responsibility. Not even the final link in the chain can be blamed, if the last of the agents to carry out a criminal order originating with the king can shrewdly provoke a foreign enemy into striking the fatal blow. The paradox inherent in this pattern is that an empowered agent who is in a position to distribute the act of violence across a number of different actors can not only appear innocent to outside observers, but can also self-deceptively shed all subjective feeling of responsibility for the killings of innocents that ensue. He doesn't need to know the sordid details. The absence of visible royal fingerprints on acts that have resulted from the king's whispered commands not only deflects social opprobrium but also leaves his conscience feeling fraudulently clean.

The hierarchical order of superiors and inferiors or principals and agents that constitutes a well-functioning political system makes collective action possible and amplifies the will of the supreme power-wielder through a carefully sequenced division of labor. The amplification and reliability of power that such a structure secures is the reason why people seek to establish a political order in the first place, even though it requires submitting themselves to its coercive power. That essential feature of political order—coerced collective action distributed across multiple agents—enhances the community's capacity for self-defense. But it also enables the turning of the political machine against the subjects who, focused on foreign enemies, originally agreed to its creation. In using the hierarchical structure of orders and commands, the sovereign ruler can also airbrush all traces of his own initiative from actions which, if made public, would jeopardize indispensable political support. In distributing the various components of his conduct along a chain of agents, not only the sovereign but each link in the chain can find some way to dissociate itself from the crime. State action, especially when it is oppressive and inhumane, becomes anonymous. It has no face.

Joab carried out David's command to arrange the death of Uriah. He did not demand a reason that would have justified the untraceable hit.[19] Although he was basically loyal, Joab was not obsequious and he deviated in an important respect from David's explicit instructions. He introduced a significant change in the way the command was performed. In recounting how Joab revised David's command, the author of the Book of Samuel enriches still further his account of political violence and the subtle way in which the responsibility-erasing chain of violence operates in the world:

> And it happened, as Joab was keeping watch on the city, that he placed Uriah in the place where he knew there were valiant men. And the men of the city sallied forth and did battle with Joab, and some of the troops, some of David's servants, fell, and Uriah the Hittite also died. (2 Sam 11:16–17)

David had instructed Joab to order the sudden withdrawal of all troops except Uriah, assuming that this would result in Uriah's death at the hands of the Ammonites. He imagined a single loss, a targeted killing of Uriah alone. But Joab did not adhere to the letter of these instructions. Instead, alongside Uriah, some

of David's other soldiers were also sent to their militarily point-
less deaths.

Joab "improved" David's command for a simple reason. If
he had followed the order verbatim, he would have necessarily
revealed to the troops that a loyal soldier was being sent pur-
posefully and gratuitously to die. Why else would Joab command them to withdraw and leave Uriah alone? If only for his
own sake, therefore, Joab could not afford to carry out David's
command exactly as it was issued. The troops might have resisted withdrawing and leaving their comrade in the lurch. And
if they did withdraw following Joab's command, they would
have never trusted him as their field commander again. In order
to protect his own authority and standing among the troops,
therefore, Joab had to sacrifice more soldiers than David had
originally contemplated.[20] To gain some control over the way
the incident unfolded, the narrative implies, Joab participated
personally in the battle. The Ammonites, we are told, "did battle
with Joab." By sharing the risks of combat, he was presumably
better able to stage-manage the situation and ensure that Uriah
would not survive.

The way in which Joab subtly alters David's instructions provides yet further insight into the nature of political violence, revealing what happens when its exercise is divided into subunits
and assigned to a sequence of go-betweens. As the original command moves along the chain, it is inevitably transformed and
changed by the agents who, step-by-step, carry it out. Obedient
as they are, loyal subordinates always retain an abiding "autonomy of performance." We have already encountered an important example of the inescapable dependence of commanders on
the commanded in the refusal of Saul's bodyguards to execute
the innocent priests of Nob. Here the relation between a much
stronger ruler and his basically loyal surrogates is more subtle.
Agents may follow the spirit of their principal's command, but
they will always seek to protect themselves from the personally
adverse consequences of which they, but not their superiors, are

aware. When issuing instructions from Jerusalem, David operates in the frictionless world of his own imagination. In the plot, as David envisions it ideally unfolding, Uriah alone would be killed by the Ammonites, assuming of course that a proper plan is designed and followed. But reality at the front is messier than scenarios made up behind palace walls. The control that any sovereign can exercise over an extended causal chain is also limited in many respects. In order to cover up David's adultery, Uriah had to die. In order to conceal this unconscionable plot, another and even greater crime had to be committed by the next political agent in line: another group of David's loyal and perfectly guiltless soldiers had to perish at Uriah's side.

Joab dutifully performed David's command, although with greater and ghastlier costs than the king had initially imagined. A report on the war's events now had to be sent from the front to Jerusalem. The finely textured narrative that relates the story of Joab's report to David is a work of art in itself. It is yet another illustration of the dazzling political astuteness of the anonymous author of Samuel:

> And Joab sent and told David all the details of the battle. And Joab charged the messenger, saying, "When you finish reporting all the details of the battle to the king, if it should happen that the king's wrath is roused and he says to you, 'Why did you approach the city to fight? Did you not know they would shoot from the wall? Who struck down Abimelech son of Jerubbesheth? Did not a woman fling down on him an upper millstone from the wall, and he died in Thebez? Why did you approach the wall?' Then shall you say, 'Your servant Uriah the Hittite also died.'" (2 Sam 11:18–21)

Joab instructs the messenger to inform David of the battlefield losses that occurred in the vicinity of the city's walls. But the way he coaches the messenger needs to be examined in detail. He tells him to divide his report into two parts, predicting that David will erupt in anger after the first installment. In this initial stage of the report, Joab insists, no mention should be made of Uriah's death; only the battlefield losses should be recounted. Joab is sure that David, upon learning of the losses, will fly into a rage, believing that they were wholly unnecessary and caused by negligent battlefield tactics. Joab's prediction of how the king will react becomes surprisingly detailed. He foresees, for instance, that David will invoke a biblical precedent, pointing out the tactical superiority of an enemy located atop a rampart, and consequently the folly of bringing troops right up to the wall and thereby putting their lives needlessly at risk. The enraged king that emerges from the picture that Joab paints seems at first to care sincerely about his troops, either because soldiers are scarce resources needed for victory in battle or because he genuinely cares about their lives. Only after the fury of the king is fully aroused, Joab goes on to explain, should the messenger proceed to the next part of the report. Only then should he reveal that Uriah, too, has died. At that point, Joab assures the messenger, the king will be suddenly appeased and complain no more.

By scripting the report to be delivered to the king in such an intricate and peculiar way, Joab aims to exert control not only over the messenger but also, to some extent, over his nominal superior, David. He had carried out the gist of David's command. But he was not going to make excuses for having departed from the specifics of the king's instructions at the cost of a significant loss of fighting men. Joab planned for the king to learn first of the losses. Only after this distressing news had kindled the king's wrath was the messenger told to placate the king by informing him of Uriah's death. In this artfully crafted scenario, Joab may have also aimed to let the king know that rumors of his plot were circulating abroad.[21] If the king's anguish at the death of his soldiers suddenly disappeared when he heard the news that Uriah had been killed, then the messenger at least would know that the king had reasons to rejoice at the death of one of his soldiers and was capable of heartless indifference to the death of those who fought loyally on his behalf.

The king's ability to get what he wanted, which seemed so limitless in the chapter's opening scene, has been fatally weakened by his furtive resort to a series of semiautonomous go-betweens to carry out his crime. David's need to conceal his hand made him hostage to the unmonitored choices of his own clandestine agents. His underlings, operating on the dark side, had to some extent become his masters. And Joab contrived to make this paradoxical dependency of a seemingly supreme ruler on his covert agents so clear that David himself could not reasonably deny it. Because the agents populating the chain of covert action inevitably retain a degree of discretion, the sovereign's high-handed authority will inevitably be compromised when he distributes components of a criminal conspiracy across a variety of different players. This is how hierarchy, when orchestrating actions that cannot be publicly confessed, is ironically upended, and nominal superiors find themselves at the mercy of their nominal subordinates. Joab's role in David's plot to kill Uriah illustrates this important and still-valid insight into the covert uses of sovereign power.

We have now seen that commands to behave in morally reprehensible and politically un-acknowledgeable ways are routinely "improved" behind the ruler's back while traveling down the chain. In another rapidly sketched episode, the narrative recounts the messenger's report to David. In delivering his report, the messenger, too, deviates tellingly from the top-secret instructions he received:

> And the messenger went and came and told David all that Joab had sent him for. And the messenger said to David, "The men overpowered us and sallied forth against us into the field, and then we were upon them back to the entrance of the gate. And they shot at your servants from the wall, and some

of the king's servants died, and your servant Uriah the Hittite also died." (2 Sam 11:22–24)

The messenger did not divide and sequence his report into two
parts as Joab had instructed him to do. Moreover, he improvised a false but fairly plausible account of how the battlefield
losses had occurred. In the messenger's version, the loss of life
did not result from a naive decision to fight in proximity to the
wall with no tactical justification. He explained instead that
the deaths of the soldiers around Uriah occurred in hot pursuit of the enemy troops who had ventured out of the city and
were being pushed back. Such a revised account was much less
likely to enrage the king than the story Joab had arranged for
him to deliver. The messenger also mentioned the killing of
Uriah in the same breath as the other losses. This is obviously
a very shrewd messenger. In deviating from Joab's instructions,
he wanted to avoid first enflaming the king's explosive rage and
then, only afterwards, calm him down by imparting the news
of Uriah's death. The last thing the completely vulnerable messenger needed was for the king to think that he, the messenger, knew that David was behind Uriah's death. The messenger
himself might have been peremptorily executed if the king suspected anything of the kind. So the messenger was justifiably
afraid that the next order sent from Jerusalem to Joab would
include his own death sentence. When he first comes before
David, therefore, he blurts out the news of Uriah's death immediately after informing the king of the other deaths. He did not
treat Uriah's death as a separate item to be mentioned only at
the end of his report to soothe the king's wrath retrospectively.
While Joab contrived to use the messenger against David, the
messenger, sufficiently prudent to avoid being so used, successfully contrived to protect himself.

After Uriah's murder, Bathsheba mourns, in what may or
may not be a perfunctory way. Thereafter, we are told, "David

sent and gathered her into his house and she became his wife"
(2 Sam 11:27). The king was now married to the widow of
one of his loyal officers who had tragically fallen in battle. The
arrival of the baby that followed could now be presented as
the birth of a child who was conceived after the legitimate marriage of David to Bathsheba. At the cost of Uriah's treacherous
murder and the militarily useless death of other Israelite soldiers, David has managed to extract himself from a scandal
that might have threatened his hold on power.

The final dialogue in the tale of Uriah's murder adds another subtle twist to the author's probing exploration of political violence:

> And the king said to the messenger, "Thus shall you say to
> Joab, 'Let this thing not seem evil in your eyes, for the sword
> devours sometimes one way and sometimes another. Battle
> all the more fiercely against the city and destroy it.' And so
> rouse his spirits." (2 Sam 11:25)

In his attempt to provide some sort of closure to the behind-the-
scenes drama of Bathsheba's pregnancy and Uriah's murder, as
well as to encourage Joab to move forward in the battle with
a sense of back-to-business-as-usual, David deployed a striking
metaphor that inadvertently illuminates how rulers routinely
strive to manipulate the public mind in an effort to dissociate
themselves from the political violence they instigate and direct:
"The sword devours sometimes one way and sometimes another" (2 Sam 11:25). The distribution of violence along a chain
of agents culminates in the perception that the instruments of
violence have an autonomous agency of their own: "the sword
devours." As the reader knows, of course, Uriah was personally singled out and intentionally done to death at David's command. But David sells the messenger a different story, describing
the sword as an autonomously moving organism, as an impersonal predator with no malice aforethought, that randomly kills

this one or that one to satiate itself. No human hand wields that sword for personal ends. Indeed, human agency evaporates in this fictionalized image of political violence. Human agency disappears within the implacable political-military machine.

If truth be told, the sword of war does devour arbitrarily. Who dies and who survives in combat is often a matter of chance, so that David is here uttering an important truth that is nevertheless psychologically difficult to accept. But he is doing so, in this case, as part of a ploy to deflect blame from his dishonorable plot to eliminate Uriah from the scene. The higher realism of the Samuel author is nowhere more pungently displayed than in the way David exploits this profound and bitter realism about the arbitrariness of battlefield death. Even the stoic repudiation of comforting illusions seems to be just another rhetorical ploy among the sovereign's many methods of covering up reality and thus achieving political deniability for his most ungodly act.

Wishing to cast the entire episode into oblivion, David sends through the messenger a final message to Joab: "Let this thing not seem evil in your eyes" (2 Sam 11:25). David's denial of the atrocity he has committed begins with the way he describes what has occurred. That he had Uriah murdered to cover up his own transgression is not mentioned. Rather, David refers neutrally and abstractly to "this thing." A thing can be buried without comment alongside the often unnecessary losses that the relentless war machine produces, tragically, by its very nature.

The story of Uriah's murder has driven home the way powerful men both gain and lose by dissociating themselves from their cruelest actions. What our author shows next is that moral denunciation of political violence involves slicing through the chain of surrogates to reveal the party ultimately responsible for the crime. This exposé was now articulated by Nathan the prophet, sent by God to reproach David.[22] Mincing no words about David's villainy, Nathan declares:

> Why did you despise the word of the LORD, to do what is evil in His eyes? Uriah the Hittite you struck down with the sword, and his wife you took for yourself as wife, and him you have killed by the sword of the Ammonites. (2 Sam 12:9)

Rather than the anonymous sword devouring soldiers randomly, David murdered Uriah personally, with malice aforethought, with his own sword. As Robert Alter notes in his commentary, the blunt words of the prophet aim at unmasking the tactics of denial and dissociation typical of political rulers. Cold-blooded murder, it turns out, even when committed at arm's length, remains cold-blooded murder. Despite all of his attempts at distributing the violence through the causal chain, David was the one who killed Uriah with the sword of the Ammonites. This is what Nathan says. To unmask self-concealing and self-exculpating modes of exercising political violence is to walk the chain back to its sovereign source and to attribute the violence directly to the one who commanded it and then dishonorably tried to distance himself from it.

Nathan's reproach elicited David's palpably sincere repentance, thereby deepening our understanding of dissociation. His very capacity for repentance reveals how thoroughly David's political existence has overridden the moral sensibility he retains as a man. We catch a glimpse of David's politically smothered moral impulses in his angry reaction to Nathan's fable of the rich man who, instead of taking a beast from his own ample flock, sacrifices a poor man's only ewe to feed a traveler. David is genuinely incensed that the rich man had no pity. The extent to which David has dissociated himself even from his own moral responses is then brought out dramatically when Nathan tells him "You are the man!" (2 Sam 12:7). In response, David becomes momentarily capable of returning to the moral self previously silenced by the weight of his sovereign persona and accepting his guilt: "I have offended against the LORD" (2 Sam 12: 13). In the same repentant spirit, David implores God to save his newborn son who, soon after Bathsheba gave him birth, fell gravely ill, supposedly as God's way of punishing the father for his sins. For seven days, David would not eat or rise from the ground. When the baby finally succumbed, the king's servants were afraid to be the bearers of bad news. But when David learns that the child is dead, he returned to his house and ate, recognizing the finality of the child's death, which he grimly associates with the inevitability of his own: "I am going to him and he will not come back to me" (2 Sam 12:23). David's underlying capacity for heartfelt grief, which we will encounter again at the end of the Absalom episode but which has been suppressed in David's plot to save his public reputation and thus his throne by having Uriah killed, makes the grip that sovereign power exerts over its wielder all the more harrowing. Had David been a cold-blooded tyrant, his quest for deniability would have had little moral significance. As a calculating attempt to dupe the public, it would not have involved David's need to silence his own conscience. Our author drives home the uncanny power of dissociation and its capacity to generate violence, therefore, precisely by giving us such a rich portrayal of David's complexity as a human being and not merely as a king.

Samuel's two accounts of royal power turned against innocent subjects take us into the core of the author's understanding of political violence. By describing in such memorable detail how the murder of innocents is carried out at the king's command in two different contexts, the author is able to present two radically distinct dimensions of political violence and to explain the way in which each unfolds. The story of the massacre of the priests of Nob explores the connection between violence and paranoia, while the story of the murder of Uriah explores the connection between violence and deniability.

The paranoid sovereign is "omnipresent." He issues orders anxiously. He is nakedly exposed and easily manipulated, while his fear of conspiracy and demand for loyalty expands without reason the circle of death that he sets in motion. The sovereign who dissociates himself from the consequences of his commands acts from a distance, removing himself from the site of violence and obfuscating his own agency. The murderous extension of what he had expected to be a "surgical" homicide occurs as other agents down the line revise his order and extend it to protect themselves.

The two episodes are in harmony with the way the Book of Samuel as a whole develops the figures of Saul and David as political personalities. In this artfully constructed diptych, the author presents us with two contrasting ways in which sovereign power tips into violence against the ruler's own subjects. It happens at times through insecurity and paranoia, as with Saul, and at times through overconfidence and entitlement, as with David. By juxtaposing these two sources and styles of political crime, the Samuel author continues to extend and sharpen our understanding of the hidden human price of political sovereignty.

As mentioned, the murder of Uriah is often seen as a turning point in David's fate and political trajectory. Nathan the prophet, who never achieved the decisive emotional-moral influence over David that Samuel had exercised over Saul, announced David's fate as follows: "And so now the sword shall not swerve from your house evermore, seeing you have despised me and have taken the wife of Uriah the Hittite to be your wife" (2 Sam 12:10). David's cold-blooded murder of Uriah may seem to us more blameworthy than Saul's failure to put the Amalekite king to death. But the denouement of the Book of Samuel does not reflect this hierarchy of blameworthiness. It ends instead with David's successful achievement of what Saul failed to achieve, namely the transfer of his throne to his son. This propitious finale of a reign that survived by means of an unspeakable crime puts Nathan's doomsaying after the murder of Uriah into perspective. Terrible suffering will now strike David's household, and interpreting that suffering as God's punishment for David's crime is natural enough. But what makes the next phase of the David story so interesting is not the way it fulfills Nathan's morally outraged prophesy but rather the way it unfolds naturalistically from the structure of David's crime itself. Nathan's ominous words—"The sword shall not swerve from your house evermore"—mirror and mock David's attempt to hide his own hand in Uriah's death by telling the messenger that the sword of war kills for no human reason. The sword that David described as operating autonomously will go far toward devouring David's own house.[23] In narrating the way sovereign power can impersonally but mercilessly ingest those who wield it, the author, whom we now know to be an uncannily acute observer of the workings of power politics, will explore structural tensions and contradictions that lie at the heart of the very project of dynastic continuity. We now turn to that theme.

THREE

Dynasty and Rupture

I

Sovereignty abhors a vacuum. Continuity of sovereignty has to be ensured and thus, when a ruler dies, the political order needs to guarantee a swift and seamless transfer of authority to a successor. Any hiatus or lapse of sovereignty, even for such critical purposes as reexamining and reforming political structures, is a luxury that no state struggling to maintain its integrity in an unforgiving environment can afford. At the incumbent's death, when the regime is most vulnerable to foreign attack and domestic subversion, dynastic lineage promises to deliver this indispensable political continuity, though only at what turns out to be an onerous price. Hereditary succession restricts the pool of viable candidates to the throne to the bloodline of the king. And the designated heir's adequacy to the role is decided by a genetic lottery that will periodically have calamitous consequences for the body politic. On the other hand, replacing a hitherto reigning dynasty, although it potentially enlarges the pool of successors, can be a shatteringly violent ordeal. At best it involves the liquidation of a ruling family. At worst, it will precipitate a bloody civil war. After having narrated the traumatic tale of dynastic change, from the house of Saul to the house of David, our writer now turns to the politically agonizing story of an intradynastic or intergenerational transfer of power. While so doing, the author of the Book of Samuel uncovers tensions and contradictions inherent in dynastic structures that reach far beyond the issue of incapable heirs to the throne randomly tossed up by genetic flux.

Saul's dynasty was destroyed before it reached the moment when a handover of royal power within the bloodline of the family would have naturally occurred. His three sons, including the gifted Jonathan, were killed in Saul's last war against the Philistines at Gilboa. That weak and feeble vestige, the puppet king Ish-bosheth, was assassinated while sleeping in his bed. It is only with David's family, then, that a sustainable dynasty is established. It would survive in power for hundreds of years until the destruction of Judah and the exile to Babylon. Yet here again, as earlier, the author of the Book of Samuel shows how the most profoundly problematic features of political life become luminously visible at their origins. His narrative exposes, already at the first generational transfer of power to David's son, the devastating price to be paid for establishing political continuity dynastically. The afflictions that grieve and blight this historically common solution to the challenge of interrupted sovereignty are elaborated through two consecutive narratives—the rape of Tamar and the rebellion of Absalom.

David's children, including the potential heirs to his throne, take center stage in the narrative immediately following the murder of Uriah. The author announces their appearance with the verse "And it happened thereafter" (2 Sam 13:1), suggesting that, beyond the bare chronological sequence, David's crime is profoundly connected with the internecine cruelties that will ravage his family. Superficially, the rape of Tamar and Absalom's rebellion fulfilled Nathan's menacing prophecy that David's punishment, after the loss of his newborn son, would come from within his household. But an attentive reading of these two narratives reveals a more intrinsic link. As we shall see, the punishment that was inflicted on David both mirrors and inverts David's own way of bringing about the death of Uriah. Moreover, the manner in which David's household was engulfed in

death and violence, whether or not it was a punishment delivered from heaven, was also, less supernaturally, an unfolding of
the imminent self-defeating logic of dynastic succession:[1]

The narrative of the rape of Tamar begins with the following report:

> And it happened thereafter—Absalom, David's son, had a
> beautiful sister named Tamar, and Amnon, David's son, loved
> her. And Amnon was so distressed that he fell sick over Tamar
> his sister, for she was a virgin and it seemed beyond Amnon
> to do anything to her. (2 Sam 13:1–2)

Born of David's wife Ahinoam of Jezreel, Amnon was the eldest
of David's sons and was therefore presumably groomed from
birth for the throne. Next in the line of succession, to the extent
that birth order mattered most, was Ghileab, the son of Abigail, followed by Absalom, David's son from his marriage with
the daughter of the king of Geshur, and thus the offspring of a
political marriage between royal courts aimed at consolidating
a diplomatic agreement. Tamar, the beautiful sister of Absalom,
was Amnon's sister only through their common father David,
so that she was Amnon's half-sister and Absalom's full sister.

The order in which David's sons were born is not explicitly
mentioned in these verses. But it is detailed in an earlier passage
that enumerates David's many wives and sons, and provides essential background to the story.[2] As the oldest of David's sons,
Amnon no doubt saw himself as the future king, naturally growing
up with a sense of overweening entitlement. Absalom was close
enough to succeed to the throne, a secondary status that presumably nurtured feelings of competitiveness and envy. Absalom
was two heartbeats away from the throne and the first heart-
beat belonged to his half-brother, the heir apparent, Amnon.[3]
To stress her place in a sibling triangle, the narrator does not describe Tamar as David's daughter, which she naturally was, but
as Absalom's sister. She was caught between her sexually preda-

tory and entitled older half-brother, the presumptive crown prince Amnon, and her protective, competitive full-brother Absalom, the third in line to inherit their father's crown.

When ravenous Eros takes hold and is backed by overwhelming political power, it brooks no bounds. This is something we have already learned from the story of David and Bathsheba. As Uriah's fate, too, suggests, the Eros of a king or crown prince can dispose of ordinary impediments to the fulfillment of its cravings with a swipe of the hand. Amnon's erotic longings confronted an even more formidable boundary line than David's: an incest taboo reinforced by cultural prohibitions associated with virginity.[4] David found a way to cover up his sexual transgression because Bathsheba was neither a blood relative nor a virgin. Had Tamar not been a virgin, things would have been easier. Amnon could have "done something to her" without irreparable repercussions. But her virginity raised a barrier that seemed impossibly hazardous to cross. Tamar was a princess. Her virginity was protected not by a simple man, such as the officer Uriah, but by her father the king and her brother the prince.

As the scene opens, Amnon, sickened by an obsessive desire to possess Tamar sexually, clearly believes that his half-sister is hopelessly beyond his reach. An ingenious solution, although one that is wholly short-term and logistical and does nothing to obviate the deeper obstacles to the deed, is suggested by Jonadab, Amnon's companion and counselor:

And Amnon had a companion named Jonadab son of Shimeah brother of David, and Jonadab was a very wise man. And he said to him, "Why are you so poorly, prince, morning after morning? Will you not tell me?" And Amnon said to him, "Tamar the sister of Absalom my brother I do love." And Jonadab said to him, "Lie in your bed and play sick, and when your father comes to see you, say to him, 'Let Tamar

my sister, pray, come and nourish me with food and prepare
the nourishment before my eyes, so that I may see and eat
from her hand.'" (2 Sam 13:3–5)

Son of one of David's brothers, Jonadab was also Amnon's
cousin. This bit of genealogy is by no means trivial. Cousins inhabit the second circle at a royal court. They live in close proximity to power, as did Jonadab, who was Amnon's cherished
companion. But they are frustratingly cut off from the exercise
of power since, unlike the king's sons who are in the direct line
of succession, cousins will most probably never attain it. The
personal unattainability of royal power that is nevertheless witnessed up close and on a daily basis may not foster rivalry; but
it can easily breed implacable resentment.

Resentment contains an element of envy, but its tendency to
seek remedial action is more thoroughly repressed. The resentful individual knows that he can never have what the person
he resents effortlessly possesses. The most he can do is to ask
himself sulkily: "Why him and not me?" and "Is he any better
than me?" Being a companion to the heirs and probably living
in the vicinity of the court, but in no way a potential candidate
for power, a cousin of the king's sons can become secretly spite-
ful and malicious. He has an intimate knowledge of his cousins,
one of whom will accede to power, and he knows from personal experience that they are by no means inherently superior
to him. When this resentful individual is shrewd or "very wise,"
as Jonadab is characterized, he cannot aspire to power, but he
can plant poisonous seeds by playing on the emotions of his
gullible cousin, offering malicious counsel,[5] and coaxing him
onto a self-destructive path.

The perverse advice that Jonadab offers his cousin Amnon
strongly suggests the former's festering ill-will. Jonadab was a
companion, we soon realize, but not a friend or ally. He first elicited an intimate confession from Amnon by attending to his melancholy and hinting that a self-pitying disposition is unworthy

of an heir to the throne.[6] The crown prince should not turn pale and mope, but should instead radiate a hearty vitality typical of those who can seize whatever they want. When Amnon confessed his agonizing fixation, a companion with the prince's well-being in mind would have tried to help him overcome it, saying to him for example: "This is too dangerous; it involves a grave sin; it is a destructive and self-destructive urge; it will not go unavenged; it will put your future kingship in jeopardy; forget her." And perhaps he would have tried to channel Amnon's carnal yearnings toward another less dangerous female at court, maybe a servant or another cousin. But far from being a well-meaning companion, Jonadab was a type we have met before, namely a political inferior conniving secretly to manipulate his clueless superior. He immediately improvised a plan not only to facilitate a closeted encounter between Tamar and Amnon but also to kindle Amnon's incestuous urges into a conflagration. As Jonadab must have realized, the script he devised for his cousin was bound to put Amnon on a collision course with Absalom, the guardian of his sister's sexual inviolability in the patriarchal order. As the predictable disaster ensued, Jonadab, assuming his motive was personal resentment, could enjoy a depraved satisfaction. He had instigated a rift within the group of potential heirs to supreme power from which he was permanently excluded.[7] Simultaneously obsessed and entitled, Amnon blindly followed his cousin's toxic advice:

> And Amnon lay down and played sick, and the king came to see him, and Amnon said to the king, "Let Tamar my sister, pray, come, and shape a couple of heart-shaped dumplings before my eyes, that I may take nourishment from her hand." And David sent to Tamar at home, saying, "Go, pray, to the house of Amnon your brother, and prepare nourishment for him." (2 Sam 13:6–7)

The pretense of illness furnished a plausible alibi for requesting the half-sister's intimate care; and the ailing son must have seemed sexually unthreatening. David acceded to Amnon's entreaty, even though the erotic insinuation of the request for nourishment from Tamar's hand was intensified by the revised form in which Amnon had asked it of his father. While Jonadab had advised him to plea for nourishment and food using the generic Hebrew term for "bread," Amnon reworded the request, specifying the type of nourishment that he wished to receive from Tamar's hand as "heart-shaped dumplings," strongly intimating matters of the heart. The verb "le-labev" used in the Hebrew for shaping and preparing the heart-shaped dumplings, has an erotic connotation that is not captured by the translation "to shape." Like the heart-shaped food that is to be prepared, the verb itself refers to the heart—"lev." In other contexts, this verb is loaded with overtly amorous connotations, meaning: "You have made me infatuated with you."[8] It is as if Amnon, in conveying his request to his father, could not contain himself, inadvertently expressing his forbidden urge in a request for care that, for tactical reasons, should have no doubt been masked as a longing more chaste. Eager for his son to recover and be comforted, David had apparently gone deaf to such suspiciously suggestive language.[9]

David's bungling entanglement in setting the stage for his daughter's rape resonates hauntingly with his own earlier crime against Uriah. He had become complicit in Amnon's plot to rape his daughter when he sent Tamar to her brother's house to prepare nourishment for him. The verb *send* was central to David's mode of operation in his plot to murder Uriah. "Sending," in that narrative, signified the king's power to create a causal chain distancing and, if necessary, dissociating himself from a direct act of violence. Now, in acceding to Amnon's request, David was employing that same power to send. But this time David's sending power became an instrument of someone else's clandestine machinations. And the causal process David thereby helped set in motion, rather than being an anonymous arm's-length extension of his royal will, turned into a fratricidal chain reaction that brought ruin upon his own household. Royal omnipotence, which has just been paradoxically depicted as a weak-willed incapacity to resist politically dangerous sexual temptation, is here redescribed as an unseeing vulnerability to manipulation by those whose motives the king or prince does not even begin to fathom. David's sovereign capacities, formerly directed deliberately against an innocent subject who happened to stand in his way, were now abused, against his will, in a sequence that consumed his own family.

Tamar compliantly followed her father's order:

> And Tamar went to the house of Amnon her brother—he lying down—and she took the dough and kneaded it and shaped it into hearts before his eyes and cooked the dumplings. And she took the pan and set it before him, and he refused to eat. And Amnon said, "Clear out everyone around me!" and everyone around him cleared out. And Amnon said to Tamar, "Bring the nourishment into the inner chamber, that I may take nourishment from your hand." And Tamar took the dumplings that she had made and brought them to Amnon her brother within the chamber. And she offered them to him to eat, and he seized her and said to her, "Come lie with me, my sister." And she said to him, "Don't, my brother, don't abuse me, for it should not be done thus in Israel, don't do this scurrilous thing. And I, where would I carry my shame? And you, you would be like one of the scurrilous fellows in Israel. And so, speak, pray, to the king, for he will not withhold me from you." And Amnon did not want to heed her voice, and he overpowered her and abused her and bedded her. (2 Sam 13:8–13)

Rape scenes in the Bible typically occur in remote, isolated places, usually in the fields. The victim is caught away from her protective male family environment with no way of defending herself and no one to hear her cries for help or come to her rescue.[10] Inverting the common pattern, Tamar's rape took place at the center of her own family's power. Amnon violated her in his own chamber at the court itself. The ostensible crown prince who lay down in feigned helplessness to be nursed and nourished by his sister had an obedient entourage at his beck and call. He ordered everyone out of the house, and none of his servants dared disobey the heir to the throne, even though they could easily have guessed the foul play he had in mind. In her desperate attempt to gain time, Tamar even suggested that her half-brother could have her without raping her, as if half-sibling marriages were legally permissible at the time. But Amnon refused to listen to Tamar's pleading. He overpowered and raped her. Sexual fixation and his inbred sense of entitlement led Amnon, abetted by compliant attendants and underlings, to commit the crime. The savagely callous way in which those wielding immense political power can treat their victims permeates what happens next:

> And Amnon hated her with a very great hatred, for greater was the hatred with which he hated her than the love with which he had loved her. And Amnon said, "Get up, go!" And she said to him, "Don't!—this wrong is greater than the other you did me, to send me away now." And he did not want to heed her. And he called his lad, his attendant, and said, "Send this creature, pray, away from me, and bolt the door behind her!" And she had on an ornamented tunic, for the virgin princesses did wear such robes. And his attendant took her outside and bolted the door behind her. And Tamar put ashes on her head, and the ornamented tunic that she had on she tore, and she put her hand on her head and walked away screaming as she went. (2 Sam 13:17–20)

In recounting Amnon's sudden change of heart after the rape, our author captures a key psychological dimension of violence. Amnon's volte-face from ardent love to extreme hate is rooted in the perverse way in which aggressors deal with the victims of their violence. The abuser begins to hate the object of his prior amorous obsession because the abused victim has now become his living accuser, a gnawing reminder of his transgression. In his refusal to confess his sin and compensate his victim for his crime, the aggressor's potential guilt is converted into outright enmity. This repressed guilt, alchemized into hatred, is what drove Amnon to order his attendants to cast Tamar out. We can almost hear the door being bolted behind her.

In this patriarchal society, a woman who had been raped was destined to become an isolated and barren castaway. Nobody would take her for a wife after she had been defiled. Biblical law therefore stipulates the obligation of the rapist to marry his victim.[11] Preferring to stay with her violator rather than be consigned to a life of shame and seclusion, Tamar pleaded with Amnon again, asking him to keep her at his home. But rather than personally ejecting his ravaged sister from his chambers, the entitled Amnon instructed his servants to do the casting out, thereby underscoring his indifference and aloofness. Tamar had to be disposed of. And our author brilliantly captures the objectification of the victim when he articulates Amnon's order to remove Tamar—"Send this creature . . . away"—referring to her with the Hebrew pronoun "zot," literally meaning "it".[12] While Amnon, the privileged prince, did not have to hide or escape from the scene of the crime, his victim Tamar was heartlessly discarded, cast out, devastated, and mournful, and seeking refuge not with her father David, who had unwittingly sent her to be raped, but with her brother Absalom:

> And Absalom her brother said to her, "Has Amnon your brother been with you? For now, my sister, hold your peace. He is your brother. Do not take this matter to heart." And Tamar stayed, desolate, in the house of Absalom her brother. And King David had heard all these things, and he was greatly incensed. And Absalom did not speak with Amnon either evil

or good, for Absalom hated Amnon for having abused Tamar
his sister. (2 Sam 13:20–22)

Absalom was a designated protector of his sister's virginity. But
he was also a contender for the throne. Playing a long game, he
cunningly soothed his sister's anguish in order to persuade Amnon that his crime would go unpunished. Absalom kept quiet
patiently, waiting to attack until Amnon, lulled into a false sense
of confidence, eventually lowered his guard.

When the opportunity arose, Absalom would avenge what
had been done to his sister. But he would also, and more importantly, capitalize on Amnon's incestuous trespass, shrewdly
scripted by Jonadab, to eliminate from the line of succession
his older brother, who happened to be the sole serious obstacle
to Absalom's becoming the next king. For the plot to succeed,
Tamar had to stay sequestered in Absalom's home, alone and
silenced. Here again we encounter the way in which means and
ends trade places under the pressures of power politics. In biblical ethics, revenge was a strict moral obligation. In this case,
too, the revenge imperative itself was instrumentalized.[13] This
is not to deny the irresolvable ambiguity of Absalom's motivations both for observers and the actor himself. His hatred for
Amnon seems palpably sincere and his desire to avenge his sister's rape may well have been a genuine motivation. But blood
revenge was also a socially acceptable pretext, serving raw political ambition by swaddling it in a selfless code of honor.

We are told that David, whose daughter had just been raped
by his eldest son and heir, learned what Amnon had done to
Tamar and was angered. But despite being "greatly incensed,"
the king remained passive. He did not punish Amnon. He did
not even reproach him. To account for David's astonishing in-
ertness in the face of Amnon's crime, early versions of Samuel—
the Qumran version and the Septuagint—interpolated into the
text the following explanation: "But he did not vex the spirit of
Amnon his son, for he loved him, since he was his firstborn."[14]

This retrospective defense brings into focus a serious problem with dynastic structures where inheritance in the male line is used to secure the continuity of sovereign power. The king, who ordinarily exercises great authority in punishing and deterring crime, is unmanned when it comes to disciplining his own sons. Paternal devotion to those who promise to make his dynasty everlasting undermines his resolve and distorts his judgment. His haughtily entitled sons, with presumptive immunity and easy access to the means of violence, are left unchastened, encouraged by paternal leniency to act as they wish.

The combination of a power to command and the exemptions offered by paternal love to legitimate male heirs can be calamitous. Yet the silence of the Masoretic text that we have before us concerning the causes of David's failure to punish his daughter's rapist opens up another possible explanation. It could be that David's immobility was rooted neither in his doting love for a potential heir to the throne nor in his political need to cover up a family scandal but rather in his loss of moral authority. After murdering Uriah and marrying Bathsheba, a compound crime that by now would have become known to the inner circles at a gossiping court, David was no longer in any position to impose moral constraints or punish the erotic offenses of his sons. His standing as an ethical figure and exemplar was in shambles, fatally eroded by his own transgressions. The resulting devastation of David's own family, following this account, was set in motion by the social opprobrium aroused by his own prior actions. Not only did the dire punishment fit the crime; it was made possible by the loss of moral authority of the father which resulted from his lecherous adultery and murderous cover-up. The coherence, psychological acuity, and persuasive depth of this naturalistic account, revealing the intrinsic connection between David's crime and his punishment, make it seem the most adequate reading of our author's perspective.

David's weakness in his relations with his sons played a further role in the ruin of his family:

And it happened after two years that Absalom had a sheep shearing at Baal-hazor, which is near Ephraim, and Absalom invited all the king's sons. And Absalom came to the king and said, "Look, pray, your servant has a sheep shearing. Let the king, pray, go, and his servants, with your servant." And the king said to Absalom, "No, my son, we shall not all of us go, and we shall not burden you." And he pressed him but he did not want to go, and he bade him farewell. And Absalom said to him, "If not, pray, let Amnon my brother go with us." And the king said to him, "Why should he go with you?" And Absalom pressed him, and he sent Amnon with him, together with all the king's sons. And Absalom charged his lads, saying, "See, pray, when Amnon's heart is merry with wine and I say to you, 'Strike down Amnon,' you shall put him to death, fear not, for is it not I who charge you? Be strong, and act as valiant men." And Absalom's lads did to Amnon as Absalom had charged them, and all the king's sons arose and rode away each on his mule and fled. (2 Sam 13:23–29)

Once again, as in the rape of Tamar, David's sovereign power was easily manipulated and used by a son plotting violence against a sibling. Having seldom hesitated to instrumentalize others, he now became an instrument for wreaking destruction on his own family. Absalom surmised that David would refuse his invitation to attend his sheep-shearing festival. He calculated that after refusing to come in person, the king could be more easily cajoled into giving Absalom what he really wanted, namely the delivery of his older brother into his hands, away from the protected zone that Amnon usually enjoyed at court.[15] To underline David's half-conscious complicity in the exposure of Amnon to Absalom's assassination plot, the text subtly emphasizes David's suspicious reaction to Absalom's request for Amnon to join him at his festivity away from the court. David asked, "Why should he go with you?," and though he had initially refused to authorize Amnon's departure, he eventually yielded to Absalom's entreaties.[16] Crucial to the narrative construction of David's parallel complicities in the rape of Tamar and the assassination of Amnon is again the use of the verb "to send." David, we are told, "sent Amnon with him [Absalom]" (2 Sam 13:27) just as he had "sent" Tamar to Amnon's house (2 Sam 13:7). The sending motion, as mentioned, resonates ironically with David's sovereign capacity for action-at-a-distance that had earlier effected the killing of Uriah. But now the king's sovereign power to "send," far from serving David's hidden purposes, was hijacked by his sons and turned against his own family.

Two years had passed since the crime and, lulled into complacency by Absalom's calculated patience, Amnon felt safe and walked blithely into the trap. David "sent" him, and he went, and he was duly assassinated by Absalom's men. At court, each of these privileged and competitive sons was surrounded by his own loyal entourage, subordinates ready and willing to defend their master and facilitate his plots. Amnon's servants, who walked in and out of his chamber at his command, locked Tamar out-of-doors after she had been raped. And Absalom's lads followed his order to murder Amnon in cold blood, committing the politically daring and dangerous act of assassinating the king's firstborn son under the alleged protection of Absalom's authority. As Absalom told them, successfully dispelling their possible reluctance: "For is it not I who charge you? Be strong, and act as valiant men"(2 Sam 13:29).

The way the royal power to command is used to forge chains of obedience that enable violence while veiling its initiator's identity is a theme that runs not only throughout the story of David's crime against his subject Uriah, but also through the narratives of the rape of Tamar and the assassination of Amnon. It reappears in the way David's sovereign power to send is turned against his family, and it surfaces as well when each son's capacity to command is used to trap and violently assault a sibling.

The precision and even the elegance of the punishment of David that Nathan had prophesied cannot be reduced to the mere retributive equation of blood for blood. The logic of retribution, as we have been arguing, tracks inherent structures of power that played an essential role in both David's crime and in its punishment. As both afflicter and afflicted, David plays the role of initiating a chain of violence. Although the results were intended and desired in the case of Uriah, they were unintended and calamitous in the cases of Tamar and Amnon.

The last scene of the narrative closes the circle. Jonadab, the arguably resentful cousin who triggered the clash by the scheme he cunningly suggested to Amnon, reappears, this time as a seemingly consoling presence:

> And as they were on the way, the rumor reached David, saying, "Absalom has struck down all the king's sons, and not one of them remains." And the king arose and tore his garments and lay on the ground, with all his servants standing in attendance in torn garments. And Jonadab son of Shimeah brother of David spoke up and said, "Let not my lord think, 'All the lads, the king's sons, they have put to death,' for Amnon alone is dead, for it was fixed upon by Absalom from the day he abused Tamar his sister. And now, let not my lord the king take the matter to heart, saying, 'All the king's sons have died,' but Amnon alone is dead." And Absalom fled. And the lookout lad raised his eyes and saw and, look, a great crowd was going round the side of the mountain from the road behind it. And Jonadab said to the king, "Look, the king's sons have come, as your servant has spoken, so it has come about." And just as he finished speaking, look, the king's sons came, and they raised their voices and wept, and the king, too, and all his servants wept very grievously. (2 Sam 13:30–36)

Rumors about disasters travel faster than the people who flee them. Before his sons managed to escape back to Jerusalem, a rumor reached David that all of them were dead. But at this point Jonadab again stepped briefly onto center stage, softening the blow by reducing the imagined scope of the disaster, reassuring the king that it was only Amnon who was dead, since Absalom had been secretly plotting for two years to avenge the rape of his sister. Neither how Jonadab learned of this conspiracy to commit fratricide within the royal household nor why he kept silent during the two-year interim is explained. We are left with the vague impression that Jonadab somehow knew that it was only Amnon who was killed by Absalom simply because he had a perhaps unwitting hand in bringing it about. By encouraging the melancholic and desperate Amnon to act, and by scheming to bring Tamar to Amnon's home, he enflamed Amnon's passion and sense of potency, fully aware that this would set Absalom and Amnon on a lethal collision course. The fact that Amnon, in order to lure Tamar into his bedchamber, had performed a script written by Jonadab that made David into an unwitting accomplice is known to the reader but not to David. To David, who was ignorant of Jonadab's role in initiating the chain of violence, Jonadab's accurate assertion apparently seemed a result of his nephew's wisdom, of his capacity to observe matters unfolding in the corridors of power. When the sons reached the vicinity of the city, Jonadab said to the king, "I told you things were not as calamitous as you thought." The shrewd and, in our reading, secretly aggrieved cousin who triggered and orchestrated the disaster was left totally unscathed. What's more, his standing as a wise loyal consoler was strengthened in the eyes of the king. Cunning and indirection are tools of weaker, resentful agents. Their disastrous involvement must be kept hidden.[17] In Jonadab's case, the concealed impact was used not only to destroy others but also to elevate his own reputation and status at court.

Throughout the narrative, our author has been making us aware of the ways in which the powerful use others in order to achieve their aims and conceal their own involvement. In telling the story of Jonadab's role in the rape of Tamar and the murder of Amnon, the author points to the mirror image of this phenomenon. Attracted less by the aura of authority than by a chance to reconfigure the ruler's agenda, relatively powerless individuals in the royal entourage strive to control the king's actions through deception, innuendo, and concealment. Sometimes, as was the case with Jonadab, a shrewd and malicious courtier will turn the power of the powerful against those who wield it.[18] Because their sinister advice is strictly confidential, it cannot be easily double-checked. The inscrutable motivations of royal advisors help explain the dark intimations of treachery that surround and suffuse political life at court, the hub of sovereign authority. More generally, great power is a magnet for deception and other strategies of manipulation. This is one reason why power routinely distorts the judgment of those who wield it. An increase in political power often spells a decrease in understanding, because political power inevitably attracts disinformation or highly selective information from those who want to use it for their own ends. The powerful will always have trouble deciphering the sincerity and reliability of the indispensable information that backroom counselors whisper in their ears, disorienting their decision making and adding to their isolation.

In the chapter's concluding lines, we are told that Absalom fled to his maternal grandfather's court in Geshur, far away from Jerusalem. Exiled from David's court, he found protection in another jurisdiction. David had already lost his older son, Amnon, who raped his own sister and was killed by his own brother. The aging king was angry at his banished son, the fratricidal assassin, but longed for him as well.

Worse is to come. But from what has happened so far, it is apparent that the killing of Uriah was a watershed moment in

David's life. Before his crime, David was at the height of his powers, moving triumphantly from one success to another. Afterward, the once secure and charismatic king descended into a downward spiral, becoming more passive than active and ending up as an accomplice to his own and his family's disastrous undoing.

David's rise and fall constitutes a great dramatic narrative, and its literary qualities have inspired a wealth of dazzling readings. Exploring the author's mastery as a storyteller, past and present readers have uncovered complex narrative techniques and structures, wordplays, and internal allusions to other biblical narratives of murder and rape.[19] But besides its literary qualities, the narrative of the rape of Tamar explores structural political themes that concern both dynastic succession as an arrangement for securing continuity of sovereignty and also, more generally, the dynamic interaction between power politics and family life. The self-defeating nature of dynastic continuity stems in part from the fact that male members of the next generation to whom power is supposed to be transferred are prone to become competitive with each other and to feel dangerously entitled. Royal families include as well a second circle of relatives such as cousins who, living frustratingly proximate to unattainable power, risk becoming venomously resentful. At the center of this volatile condition stands the father, the sovereign, whose royal capacity for imposing discipline and limits on subordinates is debilitated by his blind emotional attachment to his sons and heirs. His capacity to discipline will be even more thoroughly compromised by his grave transgressions exposed in the intimacy of familial life, thus undermining his moral authority. The particular form of securing political continuity of power through bloodline inheritance, because it fuses the personal household of the king with the public institutions of court and state, is fraught with tensions and self-contradictions. In the narrative that follows Tamar's rape—the rebellion of Absalom—the author delves still deeper into the way a family or

royal house, within which dynastic power is transferred, can ru-
inously devour itself.

II

Absalom's rebellion constitutes the longest narrative unit in the
Book of Samuel. Through its detailed and complex structure,
manifold characters and subplots, the author critically examines the deep conflict between the logic of power and the logic
of love. In the dramatic events recounted in 2 Samuel 14–19, the
price of sovereignty—of striving to seize and keep it—reached
its most calamitous heights. In Absalom's rebellion against David, the family as a unit responsible for smoothly transferring
sovereign power on the incumbent ruler's death ended up plung-
ing Israel back into civil war. Within a relatively long stretch of
six chapters, the author of the Book of Samuel meticulously
lays out the relationship between this arguably oedipal struggle
and the inner logic of dynastic succession. The first step in this
devastating sequence was Absalom's return to Jerusalem from
Geshur, where he had fled in forced exile after he had killed
Amnon.

Absalom's return was initiated by Joab, who had been David's unswervingly loyal general all along. Within David's circle,
Joab represents the voice of clearheaded and farseeing realpolitik. He therefore must have calculated that allowing Absalom
to stay away from the court too long could become a source of
trouble for David. Absalom should be brought back not only
to appease him but also to keep him under surveillance. Otherwise, unmonitored in his banishment, the angry and ambitious prince, whose assassination of David's firstborn son could
easily be interpreted as an attack on the king's own authority,
might well begin to plot subversion while slowly developing a
power base to help him carry it out. Joab also knew that despite David's wistful longing for Absalom, the king could not
simply invite back to Jerusalem and rehabilitate the murderer

of an heir to the throne. An indirect approach thus had to be fashioned to persuade David to allow Absalom's return. For this purpose, the savvy Joab enlisted a very wise woman from the village Tekoa, a few miles south of Jerusalem. She was sent by Joab to soften up the king and to elicit from him an authoritative verdict that could then be shrewdly recycled as an argument against the banishing of Absalom. It was a clever ploy and a masterful performance:

> And Joab son of Zeruiah knew that the king's mind was on Absalom. And Joab sent to Tekoa and fetched a wise woman from there and said to her, "Take up mourning, pray, and, pray, don mourning garments, and do not rub yourself with oil, and you shall be like a woman a long while mourning over a dead one. And you shall come to the king and speak to him in this manner—" and Joab put the words in her mouth. And the Tekoite woman said to the king, and she flung herself on her face to the ground and bowed down, and she said, "Help, O king!" And the king said to her, "What troubles you?" And she said, "Alas, I am a widow woman, my husband died. And your servant had two sons, and they quarreled in the field, and there was no one to part them, and one struck down the other and caused his death. And, look, the whole clan rose against your servant and said, 'Give over the one who struck down his brother, that we may put him to death for the life of his brother whom he killed, and let us destroy the heir as well.' And they would have quenched my last remaining ember, leaving my husband no name or remnant on the face of the earth." (2 Sam 14: 1–8)

The wise woman's feigned grievance, as carefully scripted by Joab, illustrates a deep dilemma within the ethos of vengeance. It is incumbent upon the family members of the victim to avenge the spilled blood of their relative. This all-important commitment of the clan is an effective way of protecting the lives of its members. In revenge cultures, vengeance is one of the highest moral obligations that family members owe to one another. Yet if the original bloodshed occurred *within* the family, brother killing brother, the moral imperative to exact revenge will transform a mechanism designed to protect the family into an instrument for its destruction. In the choreographed plea of the make-believe mournful widow from Tekoa, the pursuit of the ethics of revenge to its bitter end threatened to leave her desolated, with no offspring, her bloodline extinguished forever. If the widow's only surviving son is killed, moreover, the relatives who perform their apparently pure moral duty of revenge will coincidentally inherit the property of the father of the brothers. This material incentive taints their adherence to the revenge ethic with an ulterior motive and allows the widow to ask the king to protect her not from strict justice alone, but also from sordid acquisitiveness disguised as justice. She artfully conveys the cynicism implicit in the relatives' demand to avenge the blood of the brother by rewording their aim as "let us destroy the heir as well" (2 Sam 14:7).[20]

David was the only possible addressee for the sham widow's heart-wrenching plea. Restraining blood revenge is one of the central functions or marks of political sovereignty. The escalating spiral of mimetic violence, fueled by attacks and counterattacks, has to be tamed before it spreads like a plague. And the only force that can cauterize devastating revenge cycles is a supreme ruler exercising such irresistible power that he does not risk becoming part of the cycle himself. This is the sense in which kingship derives its legitimacy from its ability to rise above kinship.

Sovereignty crumbles when officers of the state, be they judges or policemen, become regular targets of vengeance by the kinsmen of those they have punished. The sovereign has to centralize, monopolize, and legalize retaliation for the violent attacks that his subjects commit against each other. He has to domesticate and channel the revenge impulse into regularized state punishment. If he cannot successfully outlaw self-help, if he allows private revenge to survive in some cases and retain its status as a socially legitimate practice, he must at the very least set its boundaries as narrowly as possible.

In line with this sovereign responsibility, David promised the woman that he would take control of the matter: "Go to your house and I myself shall issue a charge concerning you" (2 Sam 14:8–9). Yet the very generality and vagueness of this promise suggests that David, faced with the centrality of the blood feud to the Israelite social order, had difficulty resolving the tension between the stringent commitment implicit in the revenge ethos and the all-too-human pain of a widow who, mournful for the one son she had lost, was now at risk of losing her only remaining son. Dissatisfied with David's ambiguous and noncommittal assurances of judicial process, the wise woman from Tekoa pressed on, offering the king a way out of his dilemma:

> "Upon me, my lord the king, and upon my father's house, let the guilt be, and the king and his throne shall be blameless." (2 Sam 14:9–10)

In taking upon herself the guilt of unavenged blood, the Tekoite woman cleverly recast David's hesitation in ways that would prompt him to respond favorably to her plea. She implied that the king should not be paralyzed by the conflict between two great moral imperatives: to exact revenge for murder and to preserve the possibility of bloodline descent. He was obviously distraught about the possible guilt that he himself might incur for the unavenged shedding of blood. In this case, the widow assured him, he could be relieved of that worry because she would willingly assume the blood guilt herself. By offering the king her protection, the poor widow compelled him to reassert his own role as protector of the weak and vulnerable. After all, the woman appealed to him at the beginning of her approach by the direct and immediate plea: "Help, O king." His sovereign ego couldn't tolerate that sort of role reversal between himself and the vulnerable wise woman: "And the king said, 'The man who dares speak to you I will have brought to me, and he will not touch you any more'" (2 Sam 14:10). In offering his protection, the king reasserted his preeminence; and yet this was not all the widow wanted to hear. She was seeking an explicit resolution of her plight.[21] If the king spread his protective wings over her, what he ultimately had to ensure was the safety of her beloved surviving son, even though he was guilty of fratricide: "And she said, 'May the king, pray, keep in mind the LORD your God, that the blood avenger should not savage this much and let them not destroy my son'" (2 Sam 14:11). The king then responded unequivocally, issuing at last the verdict that the woman was seeking: "And he said, 'As the LORD lives, not a single hair of your son's shall fall to the ground!'" (2 Sam 14:11).

This was a masterful performance of personal persuasion by a gifted tragedienne, following Joab's script and extracting an explicit ruling sealed by an oath from a powerful yet initially hesitant sovereign. The ruling was elicited by her bold and iconic presentation of the unbearable price of relentlessly adhering to the revenge ethos within the family. The verdict might have been very different if presented in the abstract or by a less talented emissary.

Given what we know of revenge practices, it is clear why David was hesitant in this matter. The murder of one brother by another might not necessarily have led to the killing of the murderer by the clan, but it would very likely have resulted in his banishment and expulsion.[22] The woman's mournful entreaties extracted from the king a rather audacious precedent, modifying the traditional rules of vengeance. Persuaded by her performance to rethink the socially proper response to fratricide, the sovereign, perhaps motivated by unacknowledged paternal feelings, dramatically interfered in the deeply rooted social practice of blood revenge.

Once the king had issued an explicit verdict, it could be echoed back and applied to his own treatment of Absalom: "And in speaking this thing, the king is as though guilty for the king's not having brought back his own banished one" (2 Sam 14:13). The king incriminated himself in the verdict he rendered, since he himself had committed a mitigated form of blood vengeance within the family by banishing Absalom. At this point, David began to suspect that the entire encounter had been staged by Joab in order to lead him to such a conclusion: "And the king said, 'Is the hand of Joab with you in all this?'" (2 Sam 14:19). The woman, aware that this was a delicate moment in her appeal, since David might react angrily at being duped and manipulated, admitted to the fact that Joab had sent her while praising the king's great perceptiveness in realizing that this was the case. Having been drawn into issuing a ruling that exposed the wrongness of his own banishment of Absalom, David now turned to Joab. Admitting his fault, he commanded that Absalom be summoned from Geshur to Jerusalem. Joab knew that this was the moment expressly to reaffirm David's authority and, after praising, blessing, and groveling appropriately before the king, he traveled to Geshur and brought Absalom forthwith to Jerusalem.

Joab's scheme worked in part because David, as we are told, longed for his son and heir Absalom. Yet his parental longing did not still his anger. The king's profoundly ambivalent feelings toward this potential successor to the throne lingered, and genuine reconciliation was not reached. Upon Absalom's return, David issued an order to Joab: "And the king said, 'Let him turn round to his house, and my face he shall not see.' And Absalom turned round to his house, and the king's face he did not see" (2 Sam 14:24). In this powerful depiction of royal ambivalence, Absalom was brought to David from exile far away, but the king resented him for killing his eldest son, and perhaps also resented the fact that he longed for him nevertheless.

The result was a deeper and more unequivocal repudiation. Absalom was now being shunned not from a distance but in very close proximity to the king. His temporary banishment at Geshur seemed to congeal into a permanent condition in Jerusalem. He had been brought nearer but not closer to the king. Although present at the court, he was prohibited from seeing his father. How long would the ambitious and impatient prince tolerate this internal exile?

Absalom did not see the face of the king for two years. During this period, Joab too refused to meet him or plead his case to David. Finally, driven to desperate measures, Absalom eventually gained Joab's attention, mafia-style, by torching Joab's barley field. This was how he finally forced his way in and met his father. But a full reconciliation was not achieved. The perfunctory meeting between father and son is described in the following way: "And he called to Absalom and he came to the king and bowed down to him, his face to the ground before the king, and the king kissed Absalom" (2 Sam 14:33). The encounter was carefully staged. It had the aura of an official and cold procedure. The fact that there was no falling into each other's arms, no weeping after five years of separation and, as Robert Alter notes, the repetitive use of the noun "the king" rather than "David," suggest that the royal kiss didn't signify parental reconciliation.[23] Ambivalence persisted, perhaps accompanied by an even more bitter taste.

From a realpolitik perspective, fissures at the site of power should be avoided at all costs. Perhaps this is what motivated Joab to initiate Absalom's return to Jerusalem. But if Joab thought he would thereby mend relations within the royal household, rather than simply keeping Absalom under surveillance, he was wrong. On the contrary, the father-son rift became even more unbridgeable. Absalom was more and more resentful, having been shunned at close proximity. And now he found himself not just nearby but at the very site of royal power.

The author of the Book of Samuel traces the logic underlying Absalom's rebellion against his father, a logic grounded in the realities of dynastic structures and in the depraved relation between power politics, family, and love. It is worthwhile pausing here to recall what the author has achieved so far. For one thing, we now know that Absalom is competitive, calculating, and bold, attitudes perhaps typical for a prince high up in the line of succession. After two years of tight-lipped scheming following the rape of his sister, he ambushed and killed Amnon, the older, entitled prince who had not only committed the rape but who conceivably stood between Absalom and accession to the throne. And now that he is being humiliatingly shunned by his father, Absalom has good reason to suspect that he may be skipped over and that, although he is now a plausible candidate to succeed David, when the time comes, his father will not tolerate the idea of transferring power to him. Above all, Absalom has glimpsed something to which such sons are highly attuned—the chronic weakness of the father and his incapacity to wield authority effectively when it comes to his male heirs. Having handed Tamar to Amnon, David had then done nothing to punish his eldest son. And though he may have suspected Absalom's intentions, he yielded to his entreaties and authorized the dispatch of Amnon into a lethal trap.

Indecisiveness is a sign of weakness in politics. But the kind of mixed feelings that produce political paralysis were almost unavoidable in this case, since supreme power was thoroughly entangled with the bloodline of a single family. At the center of the patriarchy stood a guilty father who had lost his moral authority. David couldn't decide. He summoned Absalom back to Jerusalem but didn't want to see him. Smelling vacillation and incapacity for action, the competitive Absalom began to burn with impatience.

Absalom, we are told, was very handsome:

And there was no man so highly praised for beauty as Absalom in all Israel—from the sole of his foot to the crown of his head, there was no blemish in him. And when he cut his hair, for from one year's end till the next he would cut it, as it grew heavy upon him, he would weigh the hair of his head, two hundred shekels by the royal weight. (2 Sam 14:25–26)

Absalom's exceptional beauty was integral to his political charisma. It helped him attract popular support. In his case, as in many contemporary examples, hair became a site of narcissistic indulgence and a manifestation of enviable prowess. Sensing his father's weakness, he decided it was time to test the boundaries and gradually establish some facts on the ground:

And it happened thereafter that Absalom made himself a chariot with horses and fifty men running before him. And Absalom would rise early and stand by the gate road, and so, to every man who had a suit to appear in judgment before the king, Absalom would call and say, "From what town are you?" And he would say, "From one of the tribes of Israel is your servant." And Absalom would say to him, "See, your words are good and right, but you have no one to listen to you from the king." And Absalom would say, "Would that I were made judge in the land, and to me every man would come who had a suit in justice, and I would declare in his favor." And so, when a man would draw near to bow down to him, he would reach out his hand and take hold of him and kiss him. And Absalom would act in this fashion to all the Israelites who appeared in judgment before the king, and Absalom stole the hearts of the men of Israel. (2 Sam 15:1–6)

Absalom appropriated distinctly royal regalia within the court, and the king, revealing again his chronic weakness toward his sons, did nothing to stop him.[24] Absalom's self-confidence grew to an extent that he openly incited against his father. He made use of the fact that kings, by involving themselves directly in judging and resolving private disputes, inevitably risk creating disappointed constituencies. This is how the traditional fusion of judicial with executive power becomes a source of political vulnerability. To avoid the cumulative resentment of losing parties, in fact, later political rulers will begin to outsource the judicial function to legally independent courts. But the duties of the king of Israel emphatically included judging and settling private disputes. Unable to shift responsibility for resented verdicts onto others, David opened himself to populist attack. Displaying a common touch, unlike the aloof and insulated king, Absalom accosted petitioners to the court, telling them that, although their causes were manifestly just, the king would not listen and that, if he had been judge in the land, he would have ruled in their favor. He thus begins to peel away David's support by offering himself as the people's champion who will, unlike the king, hear their pleas and redress their grievances. Such pandering is politically costless and it has an effect on discontented suitors even when they have good reasons to be skeptical of empty promises. The seductive charm of political rhetoric and public overpromising is well-known. In this respect, human nature has not changed much in the course of three millennia.[25] Absalom stole the heart of the people of Israel at the city gate and under his father's nose. Time was now ripe to rebel.

The detailed account of the rebellion that follows is an astute exploration of the dynamics of usurpation. In the first phase of the rebellion, Absalom asked his father for permission to go to Hebron on the pretense that he wished to fulfill a vow he had made in Geshur. He had promised that, if he returned to Jerusalem, he would worship God in Hebron. Using religious piety as a cover and thus receiving his father's approval, Absalom staged his own coronation in Hebron, mobilizing supporters across the land. Hebron was distant enough from Jerusalem for the rebellion to gain momentum there before centralized efforts to crush it could be mounted. It was also located in the Judean tribal power base that Absalom had to secure before proceeding further. David had started his own monarchy in Hebron for the same reason. On the pretext of a celebratory performance of his vows, Absalom took with him a large entourage from Jerusalem. Unaware of Absalom's plan, this distinguished group of men thus found itself in Hebron. At this point, the people abandoned David and flocked to Absalom. The tide of his rebellion was so strong that many of the two hundred dignitaries who accompanied him to Hebron may have joined it simply because they lacked the capacity to withstand the popular wave.

When David was informed of Absalom's rebellion and the massive support it had marshaled, he was jolted from his numbed passivity. He immediately decided to flee Jerusalem and travel eastward toward the Judean desert with the aim of crossing the Jordan. He acknowledged thereby that, if he stayed, his forces would be routed upon Absalom's return to Jerusalem and that he had to escape the city and gain time to regroup. He departed the city in a state of mourning accompanied by a relatively small circle of loyal servants and warriors. In this time of devastation, running for his life and threatened by his own son, David temporarily regained his former identity—resilient, combative, and tactically shrewd. He became again, however briefly, a kind of adventurous roving claimant to the throne rather than a self-indulgent, sedentary king. While withdrawing from the city, accompanied by six hundred die-hard fighters, professional foreign mercenaries, and sworn kinsmen who had been at his side since his struggle against Saul,[26] he was careful to leave behind in Jerusalem a group of loyalists as a clandestine ring of spies who could shape events in his favor and keep him abreast of Absalom's plans. One of them was Hushai, a close advisor to David, who was ordered by David not to join his retreating forces but rather to return to the city, feign support for Absalom, and attach himself to the usurper's inner circle. Needing legitimacy and support from his father's former allies, Absalom was likely to take him in. David's principal reason for infiltrating Absalom's inner circle was to counteract and undermine the weight of Ahitophel, his own former counselor who had joined Absalom's conspiracy and who, given his cunning and experience, posed the gravest threat to David. If Hushai could neutralize Ahitophel, the young and impetuous Absalom would be left with little expert guidance and would be very likely to commit fatal mistakes.

In leaving Jerusalem, David refused the offer of Zadok the priest and the Levites to join him with the Ark. Perhaps he had internalized the lessons learned from past abortive attempts to instrumentalize the Ark, revealing the dangers of treating it as a lucky charm or portable divine insurance policy. In justifying his reluctance to agree to move the Ark with him, David made what at first seems to be a genuine expression of piety and humility:

> And the king said to Zadok, "Bring back the Ark of God to the city. Should I find favor in the eyes of the LORD, He will bring me back and let me see it and its abode. And should He say thus, 'I want no part of you,' let Him do to me what is good in His eyes." (2 Sam 15:25–26)

At this moment of reckoning, the instrumentalization of what should not be treated instrumentally might have come to an end.[27] While doing everything to survive, David was placing his personal fate in God's hands. He seemed resigned to being punished, in whatever way God chose, for his crime of killing Uriah.[28] But here again the underlying motives that drive the narrative are mixed and impossible to untangle completely or clearly. David had a second, less pious reason for locating the Ark and the priests in Jerusalem. He could use the priests, the young sons of Zadok, to inform him of what was happening in the city while he lingered in the wilderness. While David needed undercover informants in Absalom's camp, he didn't need the dangerously unpredictable Ark to accompany him on his flight:

> And the king said to Zadok the priest, "Do you see? Go back to the city in peace, and Ahimaaz your son and Jonathan son

of Abiathar—your two sons with you. See, I shall be tarrying in the steppes of the wilderness until word from you reaches me to inform me." (2 Sam 15:27–28)

Thus, the reliable young priests kept in the city nearby David's advisor Hushai could carry actionable intelligence straight from the inner circle of Absalom to David's camp outside the city.

When a king's image of authority is shaken by rebellion, previously repressed grievances are freed to resurface. On his way out of Jerusalem toward the desert, passing through a small village, David's force encountered Shimei, a member of Saul's tribe, Benjamin. Shimei felt emboldened enough by these revolutionary conditions to utter words that had been silently boiling inside him for many years. He hurled stones at David and cursed him with an aggressive ferocity:

> "Get out, get out, you man of blood, you worthless fellow! The LORD has brought back upon you all the blood of the house of Saul, in whose place you became king, and the LORD has given the kingship into the hand of Absalom your son, and here you are, because of your evil, for you are a man of blood." (2 Sam 16:7–9)

David had done everything possible to shield himself from charges of regicide. But among Saul supporters, at least, his attempts had obviously failed. His general Joab had not been punished for killing Saul's onetime general Abner. David himself, after serving as a mercenary in Achish's Philistine army, declined to fight alongside the Israelite army in the battle where Saul and his sons had perished. He had benefited from the assassination of Ish-Bosheth, had left Saul's daughter, Michal, barren in his own household, and had brought Jonathan's crippled son Mephibosheth to his court to keep him under his tight watch. For the Saulide faction, this series of actions was more than enough to stain David's hands with the blood of the toppled dynasty.[29] Wishing to defend the king's honor, Abishai, Joab's brother, offered to behead Shimei for his curses and taunts.[30] But David rejected such a reaction, seemingly resigned to Shimei's violent lèse-majesté and apparently hoping to be compensated by God for suffering a public accusation of regicide to go unpunished:

> And David said to Abishai and to all his servants, "Look—my son, the issue of my loins, seeks my life. How much more so, then, this Benjaminite. Leave him be and let him curse, for the LORD has told him. Perhaps the LORD will see my affliction and the LORD may requite me good for his cursing this day." (2 Sam 16:11–12)

Absalom's rebellious attempt at usurpation put David's concern for royal standing and personal honor into perspective. It jolted him psychologically as well.[31] At the one and only moment during his long reign when he is compelled to hear himself publicly charged with rebellion and usurpation, the usually opaque and calculating David comes across as penitent, passive, and exposed.[32]

While David was retreating eastward into the desert, Absalom entered Jerusalem. The counsel that Ahitophel gave Absalom for his first action in the city showed why David had considered his turncoat advisor the most dangerous man in the retinue of his rebellious son:

> And Ahitophel said to Absalom, "Come to bed with your father's concubines whom he left to watch over the house, and let all Israel hear that you have become repugnant to your father, and the hand of all who are with you will be strengthened." And they pitched a tent for Absalom on the roof, and he came to bed with his father's concubines before the eyes of all Israel. (2 Sam 16:21–23)

Since the king was still alive, Ahitophel understood that a clear message had to be sent that the rebellion was irreversible, that David was weak and Absalom did not fear him, and that their breach was final. Possessing David's concubines in public had

the effect of reassuring Absalom's supporters and forcing un-
decided bystanders, who were naturally waiting to see how
events transpired, to choose sides.[33]

In line with his realization that seizing the momentum in such
a moment of fluidity was crucial for Absalom's success, Ahitophel made another shrewd suggestion. He offered personally to
lead a force and attack David and his men while they were fa-
tigued and in disarray:

> "Let me pick, pray, twelve thousand men, and let me rise and
> pursue David tonight. And let me come upon him when he
> is tired and slack handed, and I shall panic him, and all the
> troops who are with him will flee, and I shall strike down the
> king alone. And let me turn back all the troops to you, for
> it is one man you seek, and all the troops will be at peace."
> (2 Sam 17:4)

Given David's dire condition, Ahitophel argued, it would suffice
to locate the king and kill him. After David's death, his supporters would quickly switch loyalties, before battlefield casualties
had embittered both sides and deepened the incipient civil war.
This was a winning strategy, and Hushai, who had infiltrated
Absalom circle as David's spy, stepped up at this decisive junc-
ture of the rebellion to scuttle it and thereby save David's throne:

> And Hushai said to Absalom, "The counsel that Ahitophel
> has given is not good this time." And Hushai said, "You your-
> self know of your father and his men that they are warriors
> and that they are bitter men, like a bear in the field bereaved
> of its young. And your father is a seasoned fighter and he will
> not spend the night with the troops. Look, he will now be
> hiding in some hollow or some other place, and it will hap-
> pen when they fall from the very first that he who hears of
> it will say, 'There's a rout among the troops who follow Ab-
> salom.' . . . And so I counsel you—let all Israel gather round

you, from Dan to Beersheba, multitudinous as the sand that is on the seashore, and you in person will go forward into battle. And we shall come upon him in whatever place that he may be, and we shall light upon him as the dew falls upon the ground, and not a single one will be left of all the men who are with him. And should he withdraw into a town, all Israel will bear ropes to the town and haul it away to the wadi until not a stone remains there." And Absalom said, and every man of Israel with him, "The counsel of Hushai the Archite is better than the counsel of Ahitophel." (2 Sam 17:8–14)

With a mixture of flattery, cajolery, and argument, in a brilliantly crafted speech, Hushai managed to persuade Absalom to ditch Ahitophel's surefire plan. It would be risky to engage in a targeted raid against David, who would no doubt hide and ambush the forces pursuing him, he argued, implicitly accusing Ahitophel of underestimating the capacities of David's men. While catering to Absalom's vanity, Hushai claimed that Absalom knew better, recognizing how gritty and resilient his father could be when cornered. A defeat in this initial step, Hushai argued, even if not decisive, would have a dangerous ripple effect.[34]

Hushai's proposal to engage in a campaign to kill all David's supporters would naturally redouble their loyalty to their leader, while Ahitophel's targeted assassination plan promised to peel them away. By suggesting that Absalom recruit all of Israel's forces for an all-out war against David's forces and supporters, most importantly, Hushai gave David what he needed most, precious time to regroup and obtain supplies. David's experienced forces, even if miniscule in comparison with what Absalom could muster, would have the upper hand in a well-planned and carefully executed battle.

His advice rejected, Ahitophel withdrew to his home, left a will, and hanged himself. What drove him to suicide was not merely wounded pride. He saw clearly that Absalom's rebellion was now doomed. He preferred to kill himself and be buried in the tomb of his father rather than being dragged and executed as a traitor by David's victorious forces.

The two armies confronted one another across the Jordan River. David divided his forces into three units led by Joab, Abishai, and Ittai, and while they moved into battle, at the gate, David issued his last command prior to the battle: "And the king charged Joab and Abishai and Ittai, saying, 'Deal gently for me with the lad Absalom.' And all the troops heard when the king charged the commanders concerning Absalom" (2 Sam 18:5). David's command to spare Absalom issued in the presence of all the troops utterly defied military logic. It would obviously be better to kill Absalom and finish the rebellion at once rather than keep him alive at all costs, prolonging the battle at the expense of the lives of David's soldiers and those of the supporters of Absalom. This was in fact the shrewd political logic of Ahitophel's previous advice to Absalom. The most efficient way to end the war is to decapitate the enemy forces. Parental care dictated David's decision to forego this winning strategy. Acting like an indulgent father rather than the king of all Israel, David seemed to view Absalom not as a rebellious usurper but as "the lad," a young son who had simply strayed from the path and perhaps could be gently restored to his senses.

David's forces soon got the upper hand. Attacked from three directions, Absalom's army was maneuvered into a thick forest and, in a state of disarray and chaos, it was overwhelmed. Absalom, having lost control of his defeated army, wandered alone in the forest:

> And Absalom chanced to be in front of David's servants, Absalom riding on his mule, and the mule came under the tangled branches of a great terebinth, and his head caught in the terebinth, and he dangled between heaven and earth, while the mule which was beneath him passed on. And a certain man saw and informed Joab and said, "Look, I saw Absalom

dangling from the terebinth." And Joab said to the man informing him, 'And look, you saw, and why did you not strike him to the ground there, and I would have had to give you ten pieces of silver and a belt?" And the man said to Joab, "Even were I to heft in my palms a thousand pieces of silver, I would not reach out my hand against the king's son, for within our hearing the king charged you and Abishai and Ittai, saying, 'Watch for me over the lad Absalom.' Otherwise, I would have wrought falsely with my own life, and nothing can be concealed from the king, while you would have stood aloof." (2 Sam 18:9–13)

Absalom's extraordinary final moments are fraught with symbolic meanings that have not eluded generations of readers. His hair, the focus of the prince's narcissistic preoccupations and the mark of his virility, became the instrument of his execution.[35] His mule—the symbol of royal standing—has ridden off, leaving him tangled and exposed, helplessly hanging between heaven and earth with no ground on which to stand. Wishing to end the battle and quell the rebellion as quickly as possible, Joab had no intention of following David's self-indulgent command. Loyalty to David's kingship took precedence over David's own paternal permissiveness and anxiety. Rather than personally defying the king's command, however, Joab would have much preferred for Absalom's death to be compassed by an insignificant and dispensable subordinate. He thus chastised the soldier for not finishing off Absalom on the spot and forgoing the prize he would have gotten for killing the rebel leader.

The short dialogue between Joab the general and an ordinary soldier, which takes place in the middle of the battle, is yet another precious moment rich in political insight. In his reply to Joab's rebuke, the soldier expressed a profound truth known to judicious subordinates. The soldier had heard the king's express order and knew that the king would eventually discover who had killed his son. Though Joab had encouraged him to seize the opportunity and kill Absalom, he would not have disobeyed the king's command even if the prize had been multiplied many times over.

The soldier felt certain that, when David unleashed his rage at the failure of his underlings to follow his orders, Joab would stand aloof, dissociating himself from the one who delivered the fatal blow. Having been heartily encouraged by his field commander, the simple soldier would then become a useful scapegoat for the general's act of faithful disobedience. The straightforward words of this low-ranking man—"While you (Joab) would have stood aloof" —should serve as a warning to generations of military subordinates who might otherwise innocently believe in the backing they will receive from their deniability-seeking superiors when the time of reckoning comes.

After this exchange, Joab understood that he would have to lead the way, dirtying his own hands by defying the unequivocal command of the king:

> And Joab said, "Not so will I wait for you!" And he took three sticks in his palm and he thrust them into Absalom's heart, still alive in the heart of the terebinth. And ten lads, Joab's armor bearers, pulled round and struck down Absalom and put him to death. And Joab sounded the ram's horn, and the troops came back from pursuing Israel, for Joab held back the troops. And they took Absalom and flung him into the big hollow in the forest, and they heaped up over it a very big mound of stones. And all Israel had fled, each to his tent. (2 Sam 18: 14–17)

Joab had brought Absalom back to Jerusalem from his exile in Geshur. But his motives are never clearly revealed. He does not seem to have been motivated by a strong desire to reconcile father and son personally. He probably did it for political reasons, to keep the fratricidal Absalom under surveillance. When Absalom's nearly successful rebellion made it obvious that the bold and impatient prince had to be liquidated, Joab did not flinch.

Absalom's helpless, dangling body provided the tenaciously loyal general with the opportunity he was seeking to reaffirm his king's sorely challenged sovereignty.

The gruesome execution, described in excruciating detail, had its own meaning. First came three digs at the heart with nonlethal means to prolong the suffering, delivered by the supreme commander who took charge. Then the death blow had to come from inferiors, the lads who finished the job.[36] A would-be usurper shouldn't be left alive. And given David's sentimentally protective attitude toward his son, Absalom had to be done to death on the field of the battle itself, though in his defenseless state, disarmed and entangled in the tree, he could easily have been captured alive. Following Absalom's execution and the sealing of his body under the mound of stones, Joab immediately proceeded to end the battle, allowing the opposing army to disperse in order to conclude swiftly what might, had the rebels been forced to continue the fight, have degenerated into a self-perpetuating civil war: "And all Israel . . . fled, each to his tent" (2 Sam 18:17).

If David had been on the battlefield himself, he might have demonstrated greater control and capacity to impose his will. But he was perhaps too old for that and, in preparing for the battle, the troops rejected the idea of his leading the way. And so he simply waited at the gate of the city to hear the results of the battle, an anxious and again sedentary monarch who wanted for political reasons to preserve his kingship and for personal reasons to save the life of his rebellious usurper son. The detailed account provided in the narrative of the bringing of the news from the front to David at the gate is constructed to show that, in these acute moments of worry, regardless of the savviness and resilience David had previously shown in protecting his throne, his apprehension for the survival of his son and heir now overshadowed his passion for retaining power.

Two runners left the battlefield to bring the news. Ahimaaz the priest arrived first and from afar he shouted "All is well," as if to alleviate the king's anxiety before he could deliver the official report. When he approached closer, bowing down to the king, his face on the ground, he conveyed the good news in a more formulaic fashion: "Blessed is the LORD your God Who has delivered over the men who raised their hand against my lord the king" (2 Sam 18:28). But the anxious king wasn't impressed by these assuring tidings. His mind was wholly preoccupied with the fate of his son. The good news of victory gave him even greater reason to worry: "And the king said, 'Is it well with the lad Absalom?'" (2 Sam 18:29).[37] Ahimaaz the messenger provided an evasive answer; he couldn't bring himself to tell the king what had happened.

The next runner, a foreign servant from Cush, who arrived just after Ahimaaz's evasive answer, also began declaring the good news: "Let my lord the king receive the tidings that the LORD has done you justice against all who rose against you" (2 Sam 18:31). He was immediately pressed by the anxious king with the same worried question: "Is it well with the lad Absalom?" (2 Sam 18:32). This time, at last, from the mouth of a professional servant, the bad news broke through, while the messenger still avoided an explicit or detailed answer: "May the enemies of my lord the king be like the lad, and all who have risen against you for evil!" (2 Sam 18:32).

David was devastated:

And the king was shaken. And he went up to the upper room over the gate and he wept, and thus he said as he went, "My son, Absalom! My son, my son, Absalom!" (2 Sam 19:1)

Earlier we encountered David in moments of calculated, stylized lamentations for Jonathan and Saul, and for Abner. Yet the pained, terse, and broken sentences of 2 Samuel 19:1 seem unquestionably genuine. They didn't serve any ulterior political agenda or goal. The sorrow of losing his son was magnified by the guilt of the father who had indirectly brought it about.[38] After all, when Absalom's rebellion gained ground, David didn't resign. He could have sought asylum in a foreign court, perhaps escaping to his ally in the north, to the court of the king of Tyre. But he chose instead to stay and fight for his crown. He implanted spies in his son's inner circle. He managed to regain time and regroup, and he designed a well-planned attack on the rebel's forces. All these moves to fend off a usurper were cast in a different light upon the usurper's violent death.

For David, Absalom was first and foremost not a dangerous rebel to be put down, but his son and heir, which is how David repeatedly referred to him while weeping. Now that the steep price of clinging onto power became apparent - the killing of a beloved son by his own army - David wished that he would have died instead of his son—"Would that I had died in your stead!" (2 Sam 19:1). The fact that Absalom was killed by David's army against his explicit orders couldn't console the king. In the past, action-at-a-distance had helped David dissociate himself from violent crime. But his formula "for the sword devours sometimes one way and sometimes another" provided scant consolation when he was faced with the agonizing effect of love, guilt, and loss.

The mournful withdrawal of the king had a subduing effect on his victorious troops:

> And the victory on that day turned into mourning for all the troops, for the troops had heard on that day, saying, "The king is pained over his son." And the troops stole away on that day to come to the city as troops disgraced in their flight from the battle would steal away. And the king covered his face, and the king cried out with loud voice, "My son, Absalom! Absalom, my son, my son!" (2 Sam 19:3–5)

The troops had charged into battle for the preservation of the king's crown and risked their lives on his behalf. Now they slipped back into the city as if they had suffered a humiliating defeat. David's personal loss overshadowed the successful crushing of the rebellion. Disregarding what his soldiers had done for him, David covered his face and continued to weep uncontrollably. The consummate wartime leader had come completely unmoored. It was the sort of unroyal conduct that, from a political perspective, could not be tolerated. Joab, the one directly responsible for David's military victory and personal loss, shook him out of his self-pitying stance by forcing him to see his paternal grief from the standpoint of the soldiers who, at risk of life and limb, had stayed loyal to him in extreme adversity. If he kept up his mournful withdrawal, the consequences for himself and his dynasty would be fatal:

> And Joab came to the king within the house and said, "You have today shamed all your servants who have saved your life today and the lives of your sons and daughters and the lives of your wives and the lives of your concubines, to love those who hate you and to hate those who love you. For you have said today that you have no commanders or servants. For I know today that were Absalom alive and all of us today dead, then would it have been right in your eyes! And now, rise, go out, and speak to the heart of your servants. For by the LORD I have sworn, if you go not out, that not a man shall spend the night with you, and this will be a greater evil for you than any evil that has befallen you from your youth until now." And the king arose and sat in the gate, and to all the troops they told, saying, "Look, the king is sitting in the gate." And all the troops came before the king, while Israel had fled each man to his tent (2 Sam 19:6–9)

This passage is one of the literary and political summits of the book as a whole since it foregrounds in the most exquisite way the profound clash between the logic of power and the logic of love.[39] The soldiers' allegiance to their sovereign is at war with the father's heartbreak for his son. If David wished to maintain power, therefore, he had to turn his back on paternal love. This is the sort of devastating choice that can be forced on a sovereign within a dynastic structure where power runs through the family, where politics and family are thoroughly enmeshed.

In the final verse of the narrative of Absalom's rebellion, the king is portrayed as back in charge. Shaken by Joab's warnings,[40] David sat at the gate reclaiming his political persona, and his troops came before him. He preserved his crown, but at an immense price. Joab's willingness to address him like an inferior— "And now, rise, go out, and speak to the heart of your servants"—reveals David's diminished condition. He seemed to have become a broken man whose family had been largely destroyed from within, exposed as it was to the relentless forces of Eros and ambition.[41] The older brother, Amnon, raped his sister Tamar and was killed by Absalom, his brother. Absalom slept with his father's concubines and David, protecting his crown from his rebellious son, had brought about that son's death. All this sorrow was predicted by the prophet Nathan as David's punishment for the possession of Bathsheba and the murder of Uriah. But the devastation was not simply retribution. Rather, it resulted directly from the deeply problematic features of dynastic succession itself, and is elaborated by our author through the paired narratives of the rape of Tamar and the rebellion of Absalom.

These two narratives express and explore the inherently unstable and self-subverting nature of the dynastic solution to the threat of political discontinuity. The expectation that sovereign authority will be transferred through the bloodline of the king places an unbearable burden on the family. The settled expectation that supreme authority will be bequeathed to one of the king's heirs leads to the next generation being entitled, competitive, and impatient. Furthermore, the entanglement of paternal love and political power means that the responsibility for preventing the self-evisceration of the royal family belongs to a father who is congenitally incapable of wielding it effectively. Given the morally dubious ways in which David had used his power as king, it is also no surprise that his moral authority began to dissipate as his crime became well-known.

The author presents his deepest insight into the pathologies of dynastic succession in his narrative of Absalom's rebellion, where the ultimate price of maintaining sovereignty was paid. The dynastic structure explored in the Absalom narrative dislodges what might be the cornerstone of the civilized order— keeping at bay, repressing, and controlling a latent oedipal tension. Undone in this rebellion was the immense civilizing effort entrenched in both the firm taboo against having sex with one's father's wives and the psychologically intolerable guilt stemming from the possible murder of the father. In the end, the oedipal drama was enacted only halfway. Having chosen political ambition over filial bonds, Absalom had sex publicly with his father's concubines. But the young usurper did not murder his father. Instead, he was defeated by his father, who possessed more skilled and seasoned military forces. When the family is turned into the exclusive vehicle for securing the continuity of government upon the ruler's death, the stakes become intolerably high. The winner-take-all nature of hereditary monarchy raises sibling rivalry among the potential successors to a fratricidal pitch. The delicate and arduous work of the civilizing project, especially the discipline imposed on intimate family relations, disintegrates under the pressure of power politics. Patriarchal families are afflicted with horizontal rivalries among brothers and vertical tensions between fathers and sons. These tensions, which are mitigated by deeply rooted social and cultural norms, burst into flames when the family is used as the principal vehicle for the transfer of such immense power. The narratives of Absalom's killing of Amnon and his rebellion against David manifest the breakdown of the delicate horizontal and vertical family structures under the strain of dynastic politics. Since the family is the centerpiece of political order within a traditional dynastic monarchy, its internal breakdown will also have a ripple effect, destabilizing the body politic as a whole.[42]

These narratives provide yet another probing look into the predicament that informs the entire Book of Samuel. The need to assure continuity of sovereignty is a genuine necessity for all human political communities. Yet the dynastic solution is afflicted with a set of inescapably self-defeating dynamics at its core.

FOUR

David's Will and Last Words

As his eventful life approached its end, the once vigorous king is portrayed as pitifully bedridden and out of touch:

> And King David had grown old, advanced in years, and they covered him with bedclothes, but he was not warm. And his servants said to him, "Let them seek out for my lord the king a young virgin, that she may wait upon the king and become his familiar, and lie in your lap, and my lord the king will be warm." And they sought out a beautiful young woman through all the territory of Israel, and they found Abishag the Shunamite and brought her to the king. And the young woman was very beautiful, and she became a familiar to the king and ministered to him, but the king knew her not. (I Kings 1:1–4)

Reduced to a shivering old man, warmed but not reanimated by a beautiful virgin, the sexually impotent king, now confined to his bedchamber, has seemingly lost control of his kingdom as well as his court. As the king's authority ebbed, the resulting power vacuum rekindled the dynastic tensions that had not been fully quelled by the crushing of Absalom's revolt. That abortive rebellion had at least taught future contenders to avoid a premature bid for the throne. A would-be usurper now knew to wait until the reigning monarch, while still clinging to life, was too physically decrepit to repel any power grab that enjoyed both popular and elite support. An aspiring usurper's window of opportunity would open only when the current sovereign was already incapacitated and moribund but, crucially, had not yet named his heir. The time now seemed ripe:

> Adonijah son of Haggith was giving himself airs, saying, "I shall be king!" And he made himself a chariot and horsemen with fifty men running before him. And his father never caused him pain, saying, "Why have you done thus?" And he, too, was very goodly of appearance, and him she had born after Absalom. And he parlayed with Joab son of Zeruiah and with Abiathar the priest, and they lent their support to Adonijah. But Zadok the priest and Benaiah son of Jehoiada and Nathan the prophet and Shimei and Rei and David's warriors were not with Adonijah. And Adonijah made a sacrificial feast of sheep and oxen and fatlings by the Zoheleth stone which is near En-rogel, and he invited all his brothers, the king's sons, and all the men of Judah, the king's servants. But Nathan the prophet and Benaiah and the warriors and Solomon his brother he did not invite. (I Kings 1:5–10)

The handsome prince Adonijah was made of the same stock as his older brother, Absalom. When Adonijah adopted the regalia of a sovereign, David, always the doting father, uttered not an admonishing word. Having never been chastised or upbraided by his father, David's oldest surviving son felt entitled to the throne.[1] Suspecting that David might nevertheless favor a younger son as heir, he decided to strike preemptively, exploiting David's politically disconnected and doddering condition to trumpet his claim to the throne before an alternative successor could be selected. In running this gambit, he had powerful supporters affording him military and religious backing—Joab the general and Abiathar the priest—who for their part wished to assure their own future influence by enthroning an heir of their choice who would presumably feel in their debt.[2]

In his ever-deepening exploration of the intergenerational transfer of power, the author of the Book of Samuel makes us aware of the volatility and delicacy of the final days in the life of an elderly dynastic monarch on the verge of death. Facts on the ground can be established, and they may have momentous and deadly implications for competing royal factions. For one thing, the contender who seizes the initiative will have every reason in the world to eliminate from the scene those brothers he perceives as rivals and threats. This is the liminal scene dramatized by the author of the Book of Samuel in the first two chapters of the Book of Kings. Two ambitious and lethally competitive sons who have yet to establish their relative positions in the coming dispensation struggle darkly over the deathbed of an ailing father who is about to depart the political stage. Our author's portrayal of this paternal and fraternal constellation illuminates once again the way political power, when handed down through a dynastic bloodline, has an inexorable tendency to devour itself.

Missing among the dignitaries invited to attend Adonijah's self-coronation were his younger brother Solomon and Solomon's supporters. In the all-or-nothing logic of dynastic succession, which needfully entails bitter rivalry between elite factions, this premeditated exclusion conveyed an imminent threat. Adonijah and his entourage viewed Solomon and his circle not only as competitors for the succession but also as long-term threats to their eventual hold on power. Better safe than sorry meant that Solomon and his principal adherents could not be allowed to survive. All of David's other sons were called to attend Adonijah's coronation feast. Their acceptance implied that they had implicitly endorsed Adonijah as the future king. He was the oldest and the boldest. As David's potential favorite, Solomon was omitted from the list of invitees, meaning that he was now a marked man.

Apprised of Adonijah's preemptive lurch for the throne, Nathan the prophet, member of the Solomonic faction, rushed to warn Bathsheba, Solomon's mother: "Have you not heard that Adonijah son of Haggith has become king, and our lord David

knows it not? And now, come let me give you counsel that you
may save your own life and the life of your son Solomon"
(I Kings, 1:11–12). Nathan's startling statement, echoed by
Bathsheba, that Adonijah is not merely plotting to displace his
father but has already "become king" powerfully suggests both
the fluidity of the location of sovereign authority and the fragility
of the process of dynastic succession.[3] Nathan urged Bathsheba
to make a last-ditch appeal to David in his bedchamber, effectively writing a script for her to recite. He obviously hoped that
David, though increasingly disengaged from worldly goings-
on, could be jolted into action by the news that one of his sons
had unilaterally staged a self-coronation, thereby depriving the
aging king of his last sovereign prerogative, the choice of which
of his sons would succeed him on the throne.

Entering David's isolated chamber, Bathsheba beseeched the
dying king just as Nathan had instructed, recalling an oath that
the king had allegedly sworn to make their son Solomon, not
Adonijah, his heir.[4] Nathan entered soon afterwards, having
carefully calculated how to rouse David's fury and thereby re-
ignite the royal potency of a king who has otherwise lapsed into
physical and mental decrepitude. By asking rhetorically if David had endorsed Adonijah's usurpation without notifying Solomon's supporters, whose lives along with Solomon's own had
thereby been put at risk, Nathan aimed to remind the king of
his yet unexercised royal prerogative to determine which son
will succeed him, unconstrained by birth order, which was otherwise decisive in traditional clan-based societies.

By emphasizing David's untapped freedom to decide which
son would succeed him and revealing how Adonijah and his
faction were effectively behaving as if David were already dead,
Nathan aimed to kindle the king temporarily back to life.[5] His
final touch was the warning that Adonijah would likely murder
David's beloved Solomon after consolidating power. The twin
appeals suggested the simplest way for David to prove he was
still alive, to reassert his royal potency, and to protect Solomon

from potential fratricide: he must effectively abdicate and, before dying, raise Solomon to the throne.

Thanks to these maneuvers, as it turned out, Adonijah and his supporters had acted too soon after all. Due to Nathan's astute and timely intervention, their brazen gamble merely roused the dying king into a last dramatic exertion of royal authority. The old man, whose sexual impulses could not be stirred awake and who had seemingly regressed into an infantile state, had more political life left in him than his ambitious eldest son had assumed. Summoning up his last ounce of strength, David ordered his loyal followers to crown Solomon without delay. A well-organized counterconspiracy, which included the military backing of Benaiah's men and the religious endorsement of the prophet Nathan and the priest Zadok, was quickly improvised and successfully carried out.

While Adonijah was still celebrating his seemingly successful usurpation of power, Solomon had already been anointed and seated on the king's throne at David's side. Mesmerized by the rituals surrounding Solomon's public coronation, the people of Jerusalem were jubilant as he acceded to the kingship with David's blessing. And as the festive sounds from within the city reached Adonijah's party followed by confirmation that Solomon had been enthroned by David himself, Adonijah's panic-stricken confederates, now realizing that they had miscalculated David's state and overplayed their hand, hastily dispersed.

Abandoned by his opportunistic supporters, Adonijah now fled to the sanctuary for asylum. The unpredicted turn of events, he knew, had put his life in grave danger. When they unfold within the hothouse of a single family, succession struggles potentially terminate in fratricide. As Nathan had suggested, if Adonijah's plot had succeeded, Adonijah would probably have killed Solomon. Nevertheless, the newly appointed King Solomon initially spared Adonijah's life, while keeping him under careful observation. Adonijah will eventually be so foolish and so blinded by wounded ambition that he will provide Solomon with the plausible excuse he needs to execute him, but only after the death of their father, who might have been loath to see another son murdered by another son.

So ends our author's artful telling of the first genuine transfer of power in the history of Israel's monarchy. While David was still alive, Solomon already occupied his father's throne, his power consolidated against all rival claimants. Woven through this riveting narrative are our author's principal themes, especially the heavy human costs of transmitting sovereign authority "unshaken" into Solomon's hands and the calamities visited on the family that bears the burden of a dynastic transfer of power. Three of David's sons were killed in the process—Amnon, Absalom, and Adonijah—two of them by fratricide. The author implicates David himself in the death of each of his sons. David handed Amnon to Absalom, sending him to his death even while nursing incipient suspicions that something was amiss; Absalom was killed in an oedipal struggle with his father by his father's general while David was floundering in his attempt to maintain his rule; and David, having failed to rein in Adonijah's self-destructive ambition, was reduced to choosing which son, Solomon or Adonijah, would have the other murdered—even though in his dotage he was perhaps only dimly aware of Adonijah's probable fate. Dynastic monarchy is a constitutional system consciously designed to ensure continuity of sovereignty. Yet the principal aim of sovereignty is to organize collective defense against foreign enemies and, in furtherance of that aim, to repress blood feuds domestically. Rather than eliminating the blood feud, however, dynastic monarchy merely displaces it. The intrafamilial bloodletting that afflicts dynastic succession represents a transfer inside the king's household of the blood feud that, before the advent of the monarchy, had ravaged clans and tribes and exposed the Israelites to foreign conquest. In this sense, the extended story of the murderous rivalry of David's sons to succeed their father on the throne clinches our author's case for the self-eviscerating tendency at the heart of the entire political project. The grim inevitability of fratricide pursued David to his final breath.

The narrative culminates with David's last words contained in his bedside testament dictated to Solomon, his son and heir. David's will, his ultimate sovereign and parental act, contains a masterful summation of the narrative as a whole, encapsulating the themes that the author has explored and interrogated throughout David's life. In their final actions, performed in the face of death, people do not seem to change much, especially men who have exercised great political power. On the contrary, aging and the proximity of death seem to magnify their characteristic virtues and flaws. In this ultimate moment, what an individual has been all along surfaces in an undiluted form, brighter and more sharply etched. This was the case with David.

The will begins with David's exhortation to his son to walk in the path of God and to fulfill his commandments so his and his descendants' kingship will be secure forever. (This is arguably a later addition to the text.)[6] But anyone who expects that this formulaic invocation of truth and justice will be followed by a genuine reckoning by a remorseful king on the point of death, repenting and warning his son not to repeat his own mistakes, would be wrong. The last will and testament quickly shifts from an exhortation to be righteous to advice that is considerably more personal. Indeed, the will is almost entirely devoted to David's deathbed hit list, instructions to Solomon about those among the Israelites who must be exiled and those who must be bloodily dispatched. This is not merely a matter of settling old scores on David's part. It is also, and more importantly, a tutorial on how to consolidate royal power. These are the *worldly* commandments that Solomon must obey if he wishes to make his kingship secure forever. To ensure that David's descendants will not be cut off from the throne of Israel, Solomon, far from walking before God in truth, must have various potential troublemakers cut down, including those who know certain truths that might, if widely publicized, call the legitimacy of the Davidic dynasty into question.

Conveying this political "wisdom" to his son and heir, David's last words brilliantly return us to the author's initial themes of instrumentalizing members of one's own community, the potential reduction of the purpose of politics to the maintenance of power for its own sake, the ruler's obsessive fear of betrayal, and morally unjustifiable acts of violence that are undertaken because they can be plausibly denied, being performed through an anonymous chain of emissaries. This is not the first time we have overheard David arranging for the murder of someone who has gotten in his way or in his face. But the deathbed lethality is striking because, this time, David's outstretched arm will reach his victims from beyond the grave:

> And, what's more, you yourself know what Joab son of Zeruiah did to me, what he did to the two commanders of the armies of Israel, Abner son of Ner and Amasa son of Jether—he killed them, and shed the blood of war in peace, and put the blood of war on his belt that was round his waist and on his sandals that were on his feet. And you must act in your wisdom, and do not let his gray head go down in peace to Sheol. And with the sons of Barzillai the Gileadite keep faith, and let them be among those who eat at your table, for did they not draw near me when I fled from Absalom your brother? And, look, with you is Shimei son of Gera the Benjaminite from Bahurim, and he cursed me with a scathing curse on the day I went to Mahanaim. And he came down to meet me at the Jordan, and I swore to him by the LORD, saying, 'I will not put you to death by the sword.' And now, do not hold him guiltless, for you are a wise man, and you will know what you should do to him, and bring his gray head down in blood to Sheol!" And David lay with his fathers and he was buried in the city of David. (1 Kgs 2:5–10)

David's longtime devoted henchman Joab was included on the hit-list that David bequeathed to his son. Here, as earlier, the motivation for an act of killing is left irredeemably ambiguous. Was Joab's execution motivated by justice, revenge, political expediency, or all of the above? We cannot be sure. David suggests that Joab had shed the blood of innocent commanders "for no cause" (I Kings 2:32). But public justifications do not always faithfully reflect private motivations, as our author repeatedly reminds us. On the other hand, as an objective matter, the moral and the tactical are hard to disentangle. If justice alone motivated David, we can reasonably ask why he waited to secure Joab's punishment until after his death.[7] Abner was a dangerous warrior who had unified the northern tribes under the puppet kingship of Saul's son Ish-bosheth. His murder by Joab many years before probably helped consolidate David's monarchy at its very inception. Indeed, David relied at every step of his career on Joab's die-hard loyalty and cutthroat ruthlessness for carrying out his most debased crimes and for guaranteeing his political survival. Joab was part of the initial cluster of companions protecting David when Saul was pursuing him. He commanded David's forces during the civil war that began when David became king of Judah. He had murdered Uriah at the king's command, making him a living witness to David's crime. And he had saved David at the nadir of his political life when he was chased from Jerusalem by Absalom the rebellious son. Joab's murder of Amasa, who had been the chief general in Absalom's rebel army, was arguably motivated by Joab's personal need to remove a rival.[8] But all of Joab's other lethal acts can conceivably be justified as helping David secure his grip on power.

Now on his deathbed, David had no more use for Joab's services. He was therefore freed to act against him, either from a desire to do the right thing at last or, alternatively, to eliminate a witness to his own wrongdoings. He may or may not have seen the assassination of his right-hand man as a way to cleanse his legacy in a more general way, obscuring the gains he had reaped from Joab's ruthless loyalty to the king and his house. The ambiguity cannot be expunged and mocks the most ingenious scholarly attempts at disambiguation.

Solomon followed his father's last orders to the end. He executed Joab promptly after his father's death, sending Benaiah to do the deed, just as David had sent Joab himself on similar missions. And here again our awkward but realistic uncertainty recurs. Was Solomon motivated by the moral imperative to impose justice, albeit belatedly, or by his need to rid himself of Joab, witness to his father's crimes and the supporter of Adonijah, as well as a know-it-all, seasoned statesman who could easily become a troublemaker in the future? Sentencing Joab to death for the murders of Abner and Amasa might also have served a dynastic imperative. It could have helped divert their families' craving for blood vengeance away from the house of David and toward the house of Joab. Political punishment, like politics in general, operates under the shadow of the double reversal of means and ends, which in this case implies the possibility of instrumentalization devoid of conscience. But it also operates under the shadow of ambiguity in our two distinct but related senses. First, observers can never be sure if power wielders are driven by moral conscience or by amoral expediency; and, second, the underlying motivations of the powerful are almost always varied and inextricably mixed. The grip of power over the power-wielder's mind and soul can shrink morality and religion into pliable tools of personal or factional ends. But this ever-present and ineradicable possibility never becomes a certainty or necessity.

Brilliant as he is in his treatment of political matters, our author stresses the ambiguity of politics not only through the content of David's last will and testament, but also in his description of the way it was executed by Solomon. The killing of Joab is located in the narrative within a sequence of actions swiftly performed by Solomon, the executor of his father's prescriptions, and in that sequence it becomes clear that what motivated Solomon was not only the need to enforce the justice that his father had failed to administer, but also ensuring that his throne would remain "unshaken," as God had allegedly promised.

The very first killing Solomon committed after David's death was undertaken at his own initiative, however, not at his father's behest. Solomon ordered his officer Benaiah to kill Adonijah, his elder brother and rival to the throne. In a formal sense, David was wholly innocent of Adonijah's death, just as he had issued no order to kill Adonijah's rebellious elder brother Absalom. Yet Adonijah's death was a predictable consequence of the dynastic monarchy David had founded and defended to the last.

As we are told, Solomon initially spared Adonijah's life. But Adonijah, apparently disoriented by the unexpected thwarting of his carefully laid plot, was foolish enough to provide the suspicious Solomon with a pretext to have him killed. After David's death, the routed Adonijah continued to miscalculate, this time appealing to Bathsheba to allow him to marry Abishag—the virgin who had warmed the shivering king in his last days—as a consolation trophy for his loss of the throne:

> And he said, "You yourself know that mine was the kingship, and to me did all Israel turn their faces to be king, yet the kingship was brought round and became my brother's, for from the LORD was it his. And now, there is one petition I ask of you, do not refuse me." And she said, "Speak." And he said, "Pray, say to Solomon the king, for he would not refuse you, that he give me Abishag the Shunamite as wife." (1 Kgs 2:15–17)

Adonijah may have thought that such a request would be viewed as fairly innocent, since Abishag was not the wife or even the sexual partner of the aging David, but merely his nursemaid and bed warmer. Perhaps he secretly assumed that he could thereby gain a foothold to renew his struggle for power since he would then be able to boast that his father's former bedmate was now his own. He may even have imagined that Solomon's mother was the right person to convey his seemingly modest appeal. Perhaps she would feel some sympathy for the dire straits to which her son's success had reduced his elder brother. She, if anyone, could influence her son.[9] But Solomon was not feeling compassionate. Schooled in realpolitik by David's last will and testament, he saw his chance and responded with thunderous sarcasm to Adonijah's transmitted request to take Abishag to wife:

> And King Solomon answered and said to his mother, "And why do you ask Abishag the Shunamite for Adonijah? Ask the kingship for him, as he is my older brother, and Abiathar the priest and Joab son of Zeruiah are for him." And King Solomon swore by the LORD, saying, "Thus may God do to me and even more, for at the cost of his life has Adonijah spoken this thing!" (I Kings 2:22–23)

Swearing to the Lord, who had allegedly placed him "unshaken" on the throne, Solomon immediately sent Benaiah to stab Adonijah to death, thereby eliminating from the scene a potential shaker of his grip on power.[10] A decent interval had passed, and political wisdom or raison d'état demanded that all rivals around whom dissatisfied subjects could rally had to be eliminated. Adonijah foolishly played into Solomon's hands. But if the immediate provocation for fratricide was Adonijah's request for Abishag, the underlying motivation was presumably the need to secure Solomon's kingship by destroying a once and future contender to the throne. David had not commanded the murder of Adonijah the way he had commanded the killing of Joab. But it was an act fully in the spirit of David's last will and testament. It conformed to his precepts for consolidating power by eliminating those suspected of having the capacity to unsettle the throne.

After sending Benaiah to murder Adonijah, as already mentioned, Solomon turned his attention to Adonijah's military and religious supporters, Joab and Abiathar. They, too, had to be removed from the scene.

Abiathar the priest, the leading religious figure in Adonijah's conspiracy, was banished into exile in a small village. Solomon was not paranoid like Saul. He would not kill priests. They posed no significant threat and could simply be removed from the cultic center and be done with. Moreover, as witness to *Saul's* greatest crime (the murder of the priests of Nob), Abiathar could potentially add to the legitimacy of the Davidic line—quite unlike Joab who was, much more troublingly, witness to *David's* greatest crime.

Having heard that Solomon was moving swiftly and had already killed Adonijah and exiled Abiathar, Joab was experienced enough to understand that he was next in line. He had been in power for many decades. He knew that the lethal factional conflicts normally accompanying dynastic succession tend to end in the murder of the leaders of the losing faction: "And the news reached Joab, for Joab had sided with Adonijah, though with Absalom he had not sided, and Joab fled to the Tent of the LORD, and he grasped the horns of the altar" (I Kings 2:28–29).[11] Solomon "sent" his general to kill Joab, and Joab, refusing to leave the asylum of the sanctuary, challenged Benaiah to kill him at the altar. Benaiah who hesitated to perform what might be a sacrilegious act, reported back to Solomon. The king ordered him to kill Joab even at the site of the altar:

> And the king said, "Do as he has spoken, and stab him and bury him, and you shall take away the blood that Joab shed for no cause, from me and from my father's house. And the LORD will bring back his blood guilt on his own head, for he stabbed two men more righteous and better than himself and he killed them by the sword, unbeknownst to my father

David —Abner son of Ner, commander of the army of Israel, and Amasa son of Jether, commander of the army of Judah. And their blood will come back on the head of Joab and on the head of his seed forever, but for David and his seed and his house there will be peace evermore from the LORD." And Benaiah son of Jehoiada went up and stabbed him and put him to death, and he was buried at his home in the wilderness. And the king put Benaiah son of Jehoiada in his stead over the army, and Zadok the priest did the king put instead of Abiathar. (I Kings 2:31–35)

The language justifying the killing of Joab in the midst of the sanctuary is shot through with moral and religious norms, notably the belief that blood shed today can wipe away the stain of blood shed in the past. Yet here again the author forces us to face the question of the relation between justification and motivation, leaving open the question of their convergence or divergence. The larger context reveals the extent to which the killing of Joab served political purposes. It is true that the killing of Abner by Joab was committed without David's knowledge. He did not authorize it, but neither had he admonished, much less punished, Joab after learning what he had done. Joab acted with impunity just so long as David needed his help and support.

The artfully crafted context in which the narrative locates Solomon's initial moves to consolidate his grip on power, extinguishing Adonijah and his supporters—including Joab—raises the question: would Solomon have had Joab killed had he still needed his murderous services? However grave the crimes with which he was charged, moreover, would Joab have been killed had he not played a role in Adonijah's conspiracy? The last lines of the narrative bring us back to one of our author's central themes: the invocation of justice to palliate, excuse, and rationalize conduct undertaken for reasons of pure political expediency is a possibility that haunts all genuine political action.

Before turning to focus on Shimei, the second target on David's hit list, it will be worthwhile to linger for a moment over the figure of Adonijah. The portrait of that figure is one of the jewels left to us by the author of the Book of Samuel, and though it is not the main thrust of our argument—Adonijah was a relatively minor figure in the story—it would be a shame not to look more closely at this precious character portrait to discover what it can tell us about political ambition roused by the lure of sovereign power. Adonijah was a handsome man, the brother of Absalom, who thought he had learned the lessons of his elder brother's failure. As the oldest surviving son, he behaved as the future king but, unlike Absalom, he kept his impatience under control. He waited till the moment when the king seemed physically unmanned and politically disengaged. But he sorely misjudged David's condition and, though he rallied considerable support, his gamble proved fatal. Ironically, the gamble itself was the reason for his calamitous failure, since Nathan used it to awaken David from his senescent slumber and to trigger the king's last decisive political act. Adonijah barely survived his failed coup; and Solomon temporarily spared his life. It might have seemed that he would have understood the precariousness of his position as a defeated but still surviving contender for the throne. But Adonijah refused to abandon all hope. He apparently thought that he had found a way to reenter the contest for power, beseeching Solomon's mother to secure Abishag as his wife. The interpreter of such an implausible ploy wonders what Adonijah actually thought. [12] Was he completely oblivious to the possibility that his request would ignite the suspicions of Solomon, a king who was naturally waiting for his rival to provide him a reason to remove him from the scene? He miscalculated again, and this slipup cost him his life. What this story reveals is the addictive nature of power, its blinding force, and the heavy price it compels its obsessive seekers to pay. All of us, somewhere in the corridors of power, either low or high, have encountered Adonijah-like figures. They embody the unseeing stupidity of the ambitious, especially when they attempt to be clever.

The second important target on David's hit list was Shimei. Unlike Joab, Shimei was neither a coconspirator in the Adonijah plot nor an important figure in David's life. Instead, he was a marginal man, an angry Benjaminite who had retained his loyalty to the house of Saul even after it had been decimated. When David was running for his life escaping Jerusalem at the time of Absalom's rebellion, he encountered Shimei, who cursed him loudly, barking that "all the blood of the house of Saul" was on David's head (2 Sam 16:8). As we have seen, David had gone to great extremes to distance himself from the deaths of Saul and all his heirs, deaths which, whatever their cause, substantially tightened his own grip on power. So he cannot have welcomed Shimei's taunts. Indeed, Shimei's public proclamation that David was a usurper who had murdered his predecessor, extinguished his line, and stolen his throne was probably the last thing he wanted to hear. At the time, David's loyal officer Abishai, the brother of Joab, wanted to kill Shimei for casting aspersions on David's legitimacy. But David, in what seemed a genuine moment of humility, reproached Abishai with the following harsh words:

> "What do I have to do with you, O sons of Zeruiah? If he curses, it is because the LORD has said to him, 'Curse David,' and who can say, 'Why have you done this?'" And David said to Abishai and to all his servants, "Look— my son, the issue of my loins, seeks my life. How much more so, then, this Benjaminite. Leave him be and let him curse, for the LORD has told him. Perhaps the LORD will see my affliction and the LORD may requite me good for his cursing this day." (2 Sam 16:10–12)

This passage, which we have cited once before, recounts or seems to recount a moment of acceptance and reckoning on David's part. It feels as if the thick shell of David's opaque and

calculating public personality is being penetrated and his complexity as a human is being revealed. Absalom's rebellion may
have seemed to David the just punishment for the murder of
Uriah that Nathan had prophesied. That might explain why
David responded so nonaggressively to Shimei's quite different
charge that he was a regicide and usurper. If he could tolerate
such excoriation, perhaps God would forgive his trespasses.

After the rebellion had been crushed and David was on his
way back to Jerusalem, Shimei was among the first to appeal to
him for mercy. He now feared that David, having survived this
revolt, would take revenge and kill him. True to himself, Abishai
again offered to put Shimei to death for asserting that David
had consolidated his power by obliterating a rival dynasty. But
David reproached Abishai a second time:

> And Abishai son of Zeruiah spoke out and said, "For this
> should not Shimei be put to death? For he cursed the LORD's
> anointed." And David said, "What do I have to do with
> you, sons of Zeruiah, that you should become my adversary
> today? Should today a man of Israel be put to death? For I
> surely know that today I am king over Israel." And the king
> said to Shimei, "You shall not die." And the king swore to
> him. (2 Sam 19:22–24)

This gesture of victor's magnanimity casts a somewhat different
light on David's surprising leniency toward Shimei's earlier accusation of regicide. Instead of expressing sincere penitence for
his sins, his tolerance of Shimei's curses may have been designed
to reconcile the Benjaminites to David's return to power. By
brushing aside petty considerations of honor and status, moreover, David may have aimed to dissociate himself not only from
Abishai but from Joab as well when he exclaimed, "What do I
have to do with you sons of Zeruiah," referring to the brothers who represent irreconcilable hostility to all David's enemies
throughout the story. This was David's characteristic political
style. While using these ruffians on secret missions, he managed

to dissociate himself from them publicly. In ordering Solomon to execute Joab for the crimes he had performed, David put the finishing touches on the dissociation project central to his exercise of royal power: David *had nothing to do* with the sons of his sister Zeruiah!

David's final words, ordering Solomon to send Shimei into the grave splattered with blood, should alert us to the impossibility of completely disentangling moral obligation and political calculation. Coeval with the emergence of genuinely political life, it turns out, is the lingering possibility that the morality publicly invoked by powerful rulers might be a mere tool used for immoral or amoral ends. Yet the exact degree to which morality, incessantly invoked by those in power, is being instrumentalized remains impossible to ascertain. Shimei was a minor figure who roared his imprecations when David was weak and fleeing. Later when the tables had turned, David swore to him that he would not be killed. We have no reason to doubt the sincerity of David's expression of humility and magnanimity, articulated in contrast to the calculating vengefulness of Zeruiah's sons, Joab and Abishai. But David's last will, instructing Solomon to put Shimei to death, without having rebutted Shimei's charges or explaining why he was breaching the magnanimous promise he had made, makes his motivations both harder to read and more complex.

David's humility and magnanimity may have been fleeting moments that did not define his core or sincere personal impulses that were ultimately silenced by the imperatives of office or they may have been another example of moral theater, one of many that David performed during his life as a sovereign.[13] Thus, the author's choice to end David's life with his order to kill Shimei: "bring his gray head down in blood to Sheol!" (I Kings 2:9–10) refocuses our attention once again on many of the book's central themes: the essential ambiguity of political motivation and political action, the inherent pettiness of the power game, the tendency for political power, once attained, to be redirected toward retaining political power, the ruler's need to manipulate his public image, the centrality of blame-avoidance and blame-shifting to the exercise of sovereignty, how the possession of great power affects the ends that power wielders pursue, and the way power tends to imprison those who most ardently seek it. These are David's very last words. They convey to his son and successor how a newly enthroned king who loves and respects his recently deceased father is expected to behave. This finale was also the author's way of ending his reflections on politics by recounting David's last days in a way that brings us back to the themes he has investigated throughout the narrative—the inscrutability and ambiguity of political motivation, the double reversal of means and ends, the arts by which rulers disseminate an official version of events, the shedding of even the most basic moral inhibitions in the struggle for political and physical survival, a half-crazed obsession with rivals to power, an overheated fear of betrayal, the political deniability made possible by action-at-a-distance, the corrupting indulgence with which royal fathers treat their sons and heirs, and the way blood feuds among clans and tribes, largely repressed by sovereign authority, resurface inside the sovereign's own household, to disastrous effect.

Conclusion

The identity of our immensely astute observer of politics and the greatest author ever to write in the Hebrew language remains unknown. This is a most frustrating fact given the magnitude of the debt that we owe whoever crafted these riveting narratives for the wisdom and the insight that we gain from a close and attentive reading of the Book of Samuel. But even though we cannot identify the author, we can safely speculate about some aspects of the environment and the conditions under which this extraordinary book was composed. The author was not a high functionary in some political apparatus of the time, since the outlook expressed in the narrative is that of an outsider. Nor was the author a spokesman for a certain faction, be it the Davidic party or the Saulide party or a representative of the old elite of elders and judges marginalized by the rise of monarchy. The author was not a scribal courtier either. No court would allow the composition of such an unflattering official history of its beginnings and such a complexly ambiguous depiction of its founding father. Its systematic ambiguity, contrary to all hagiographic conventions, is what gives such astonishing force to the author's account.[1] The book is thus not a political manifesto, a piece of agitprop aimed at supporting or advancing a particular political sect, party, or person. It is rather a book *about* politics in which its author's distance from all political factions allowed for the creation of a genuine masterpiece of political thought woven ingeniously into a naturalistic retelling of dramatic historical events.

The author does not seek to represent God's point of view either, given that God himself is among the dramatis personae of the book and is obviously not its concealed author. Nevertheless, God has to find his place in the new order of politics that he self-effacingly accepts, even though it was created against his will. Like a retired boss, the one who used to be king, God substantially redefined his own role at the moment his people demanded a human, and therefore humanly flawed, king. When the Israelite monarchy was first established, God compared his people's headstrong decision to reject his kingship and replace it with a unified dynastic monarchy to previous episodes when they worshipped other gods. He also warned the people that he would no longer come to their rescue when they eventually begged to be saved after they were predictably abused by their worldly monarch. It was as if he told them: "You wanted me out. Let it be, but do not ask me back." This was not quite the way God eventually behaved, to be sure. He did not exactly withdraw into the desert.

Through his prophet Samuel, we are told, God made Saul king—the kind of king who in no way resembled a god. And he then commanded the new king to initiate a holy war unnecessary for the immediate political needs of the community. Subsequently, God rejected Saul and replaced him. He next chose David, made an everlasting covenant with him, and punished him when he sinned. This was by no means a full retirement from the political stage. But there was a dramatic change in God's mode of operation in comparison with the time when he had been the one and only sovereign. For one thing, God no longer played a decisive battlefield role. More significantly, his interventions became deeply intertwined with, even indistinguishable from, the natural course of events. Saul's internal collapse, his military defeat by the Philistines, his replacement by the charismatically savvy David who survived as a fugitive and guerrilla leader—all these occurrences unfold in an atmosphere suffused with contingency and cliff-hanging suspense and could easily be imagined without any divine activity or plan. David's punishment for adultery and murder, as foretold by the prophet Nathan, beautifully tracks the natural development and degeneration of dynastic politics. In our author's narrative, no manna has fallen from heaven, and no Red Sea was miraculously split apart. God's interventions have become thoroughly political.[2] They follow and reveal the imminent logic of politics, as if to say that divine providence and reward and punishment in politics are endogenous to politics itself.

Obviously conversant with the workings of royal and tribal politics, Samuel's author, though not an active agent of a political machine, must have resided at court or have once been part of the political world itself. To be sure, the author's acquaintance with political life was not confined to intimate familiarity with what actually happened in Saul's and David's courts. Much of what the author reported was no doubt the fruit of a wondrously fertile imagination. It is indeed clear that some of the details in the story are the product of sheer artistic inventiveness since they could not have been known to any author, however at home in the corridors of power. One example is the marvelously detailed account of what Joab said to the messenger sent to inform David about the death of Uriah and of the way the messenger subtly altered the message when conveying the report to David himself. Such specifics—like references throughout the narrative to the distinctive internal lives of the characters—were private details with which no one besides the individuals personally involved could possibly have been acquainted. The author wrote in the tradition of an all-knowing narrator, adding fictionalized material to what was presumably a faithful though skeletal rendering of historical events. When we refer to the author's firsthand acquaintance with political life, therefore, we don't have in mind only or even primarily insider information but mainly a deep grasp of political life.

The author's basic outlook on political life is rooted in the book's account of the origins of politics. Sovereignty was established and embraced in response to pressing, life-or-death human concerns and needs. The capacity to organize collective action through the authority to tax and draft is necessary for any community that strives to survive in a hostile and unforgiving environment. A loose-knit confederation of disputatious tribes was especially vulnerable at its frontiers, where territorial disputes with neighboring peoples were most acute. Such vulnerability explains the legitimate aspiration to overcome strife inside a tribal confederacy and to enforce unity. Yet this rationale for pooling collective resources by centralizing the power to command is fraught with a deep contradiction that lies at the core of political life and that our author brings into focus with exceptional artistry and theoretical force.

If the sovereign is powerful enough to protect the people against hostile neighbors, he will also be powerful enough to abuse the people for reasons having nothing to do with collective security. The possibility that rulers will betray the ruled is inherent to the nature of rule itself and may or may not be rooted in the personal psychology of those who inhabit high office. Pointing to this inherent contradiction in the human political project did not lead the author to recommend abolishing sovereign authority or reverting back to the divine anarchy or the weak and decentralized social order that preceded the monarchy, when laws went unenforced and every man did what was right in his own eyes (Judges 21:26).

Focusing on sovereignty's dark sides does not lead the author to reject sovereignty as such. The book is not a policy brief or proposal for a model constitution. The political horizons of the author of Samuel did not reach to suggesting reforms or offering alternative institutional mechanisms. Moreover, the many lessons that can be drawn about politics from the Book of Samuel are unrelated to the advocacy of worthy and inspiring political ideals. The book does not preach or endorse the rule of law,

care for the poor, civic participation, or the legal equality of subjects in a covenantal political constitution. Instead, the author
turned a penetrating gaze onto the punishing costs of sovereign
power as such.

The illuminating force of the book's fine-grained phenomenology of power, therefore, takes us beneath debates about forms
of government and public ideals, and reaches a more primary
and elemental level of politics. This is what makes it relevant
to the study of political power whenever it is practiced, regardless of the particular program or ideology that sovereign government serves. Its anatomy of sovereignty applies not only to
dynastic kingship in a tribal society but, with suitable modifi-
cations, illuminates important features of every political order,
including the welfare state, the liberal state, and so forth.

At the root of the structure of politics unveiled in the narratives of the Book of Samuel lies a double reversal of means
and ends that is immanent to sovereign power. Power is an
indispensable tool needed for a vital collective good. It must
therefore be organized and cultivated. But the sovereign who
has gained it and those around him who compete for it do not
see supreme political power exclusively from the public's point
of view, as a means for organizing collective defense. The seekers and wielders of sovereign authority inevitably see it from a
more personal perspective. The privileges and status of the highest political office can be intoxicating, transforming sovereign
authority all too easily into an end-in-itself, a stand-alone goal
which becomes the very raison d'être of those seeking to gain
or maintain it. It is no secret that many power wielders end up
using much of the power they have attained to help them stay in
power.[3] This perverse conversion of a means into an end afflicts
a wide range of political regimes. It is therefore fair to say that
it presents a structural vulnerability of politics as such.

The second reversal of means and ends, deeply connected
to the first, also looms disquietingly over politics in all its incar-
nations. It involves the conversion of genuine ends such as the

sacred, love, loyalty, and moral obligation into means in the hands of power wielders who, above all, seek to maintain their rule. This is how the instrumentalization of what should not be instrumentalized becomes a defining and degrading feature of political action. It has a corrosive effect not only on those aspiring to seize power but also on those who, after seizing power, fall into its vise-grip. It can and frequently does contribute to an environment of alienation, mistrust, and paranoia that naturally erupts in violence.

This double reversal of means and ends also occurs in other human realms. Money seems to be another necessary tool that suffers from a similarly perverse tendency to turn into something desired for its own sake. But in the case of sovereign power, such an inversion can be immensely consequential. Among the effects of these twin reversals, subtly explored by our author, is the way in which political actions become systematically ambiguous.

The environment in which politics unfolds is defined by the inability of subjects to know with any certainty if the justifications offered by rulers accurately reflect or deceptively conceal their underlying motivations. But the ambiguity of political action, as dramatized in the stories of Saul and David, cuts even deeper than this. It is difficult to disentangle the moral and the tactical in the action of political rulers not only because we cannot read their minds but also because obligation and calculation, the moral and the instrumental, are very likely to be juxtaposed and fused in a sovereign ruler's mind. Multiple and mixed motives mean that "unmasking" the supreme ruler by exposing cynical plots lurking behind a pseudomoral facade is based on an overly dichotomous understanding of the relation between motivation and justification. The idea that sovereign power is inevitably exercised under the shadow of this systematic ambiguity is another striking and still resonant theme of our author's political thought.

The public's uncertainty about the ruler's motivations are matched by an epistemic deficiency afflicting the ruler himself.

Aloof and distant, he is dependent on others to provide him with a picture of reality and, given his immense power to bestow benefits and harms, members of his close circle and others, too, tend to manipulate the information they provide him in the service of their own private or factional interests. Disconnect and vulnerability to disinformation can easily deepen, moreover, as a result of the sovereign's instrumentalization of his followers. The consequence, in such a case, can be gnawing suspicion and a complete breakdown of trust. The trite observation that even paranoids have enemies does not diminish the role of pathologically exaggerated distrust in distorting the judgment of those who exercise sovereign power. Encircled by those who covet or envy his position and sometimes unjustifiably projecting his own hunger for power onto them, the sovereign can easily be overtaken by conspiratorial fears and insecurities, states of mind that powerfully distort his mode of operation. By virtue of its peerless preeminence and solitary remoteness, therefore, sovereign power can burden its wielder, as in Saul's case, even more than its subjects. Endemic to great political power in all its forms, the ruler's isolation brings us to another of our author's key insights, this time into the sources of political violence.

The twenty-three verses that the author devotes to the massacre of the priest of Nob at the hands of Saul and the chapter that narrates the murder of Uriah by David provide startling accounts of two distinct faces of violence. The first draws attention to the relationship between violence and insecurity and the second to the roots of violence in entitlement. Saul's paranoia leads him to distrust everyone around him, suspecting that his officers and retainers are loyal only opportunistically and that they could easily abandon him for a militarily more successful rival. Deprived of ordinary sanity checks by the very aloofness of his royal office, he casts himself as an unfairly abused victim even while he is engaged in an aggressive attempt to track David down and kill him. His maudlin self-pity, tellingly, is a prelude to violence. Infuriated by the inability of his forces to capture

David, he lashes out against Abimelech and the wholly innocent priests of Nob, using a foreign mercenary who is devoid of religious scruples and tribal loyalty to do the killing that Saul's own troops—illustrating the dependence of rulers on their armed retainers—righteously refuse to commit. Saul's crime resulted from some central features of sovereign power, especially the endemic isolation that comes from a relentless instrumentalization of those around the sovereign who remain perpetually subject to his whim. That supreme power functions as a magnet for lies is another reason why the supremely powerful can easily fall into a state of paranoid suspiciousness. In Saul's case, the acute fear of being betrayed by his own agents naturally resulted from the isolation chamber in which the wielder of supreme executive power is enabled or compelled to live.

The danger posed by sovereign power when it becomes existentially insecure resonates across the political spectrum in all its modes and forms. The detailed yet spare narrative of the massacre of the priests of Nob illustrates the potential consequences of such a condition. Specific to paranoia is the lack of a defined and delimited object of dread. This is what makes a paranoid mental condition easy to manipulate, redirect, and inflate. Violence loosed in conditions of paranoia will naturally escalate into overkill, sweeping up innocent and guilty subjects alike, since it roams in an unbounded and uncontrolled vicious cycle of burning rage, bogus victimhood, and baseless suspicion.

Another essential feature of politics and the root of its irresistible appeal is the way hierarchical structures facilitate the possibility of collective action. Sovereign bodies organize hierarchical chains of command and establish a meticulous distribution of labor across diverse agents, thus magnifying the aggregate effectiveness of individuals by forging them into a cohesive group able to act in concert. When the sovereign turns the political machine against his own subjects, however, these same essential structures, so vital for publicly beneficial collective action, allow the sovereign to escape any personal responsibility for the infliction of publicly unjustifiable violence. The long chain at the sovereign's disposal facilitates and thus encourages crime by distributing the commission of criminal acts across many agents, each contributing to a multitiered distribution of labor, diffusing responsibility, frustrating accountability, and granting the supreme ruler deniability and impunity. In the author's narrative of the murder of Uriah, these themes are masterfully explored through the power of David to "send" and act at a distance. The dissociation enabled by the obscuring of agency finds its most penetrating expression in David's statement, one of the greatest literary portrayals ever presented of political deniability, "for the sword devours sometimes one way and sometimes another."

Delving deeper into the microworkings of power, the narrative excavates another potentially perverse consequence of acting through an extended chain of agents. It brings to light the relative independence of the links in the chain and the way in which subordinates, while attempting to protect themselves and "improve" upon the sovereign's commands, have a tendency to increase the lethality of the crime they have been detailed to carry out. Our author illuminates the way these subordinate links in the ruler's chain of command, because they operate in the dark world of state secrets where possibilities for monitoring are radically reduced, can hold their sovereign hostage even as they carry out his crimes. This complex and fine-grained analysis of deniability and dissociation, distilled from observing the very origins of sovereignty and collective political action, reverberate chillingly up to the present day.

Continuity of sovereignty is another deadly serious political concern. The need to assure the smooth transfer of power rests on a sincere anxiety stemming from a community's vulnerability, during an interregnum, to foreign attack and domestic civil war. Without an agreed-upon succession formula, no state can be considered even minimally stable or secure. Yet, the dynastic way of insuring the continuity of sovereignty, like the necessity of sovereignty itself, is fraught with self-defeating potential.

The author of the Book of Samuel does not argue against the dynastic solution to the continuity problem. His book focuses, instead, on the costs that centralizing political power inflicts not only on the ruled but also on the ruler and his children, exploring the impact of mingling family love and political ambition and the ways in which the core members of a royal dynasty can be crushed as their family becomes a vehicle for the transfer of sovereignty. The problem of political continuity, like the problem of collective action in general, has to be solved. But no plausible answer can be given to such a deep social problem without engendering other problems, of no lesser gravity and intractability.

In the second period of David's reign, after Uriah's murder and the subsequent weakening of the king's political prestige, the price of sovereignty is paid, sequentially, by Tamar, Amnon, Absalom, and Adonijah. And no doubt the ultimate expression of the cost that sovereignty exacts upon its wielders is David's heartfelt cry: "My son, Absalom! My son, my son, Absalom! Would that I had died in your stead! Absalom, my son, my son!" (2 Sam 19:4). The civil war between Israelite tribes, which the Unified Monarchy was meant to suppress, had reappeared within the king's own household. Similarly, lethal rivalry between the Saulide and the Davidic dynasties segues smoothly into lethal rivalry inside David's house. So the dynastic solution to the continuity problem displaced rather than resolved the problem of violent transfers of power. The drivers of the fratricidal and conspiratorial violence that occupy this portion of the narrative are the entitlement and impatience inculcated into potential royal heirs, the bitter envy of close relatives excluded from the succession, and the calculations of rival military and religious officials of the king.

Admittedly, the rape of Tamar, the ambush of Amnon, and the conspiracy of Absalom may seem less relevant to political power in nondynastic systems of rule than other parts of the Book of Samuel. Indeed, democratic systems for the alternation in office of rival parties can be understood as a way to discipline the factional struggle for supreme power in a way that does not require the winning party to kill the leaders and chief adherents of the party that loses. The eventual separation of judicial and executive power, the fusion of which made David vulnerable to Absalom's rebellion, had a similarly stabilizing effect. Yet despite such institutional innovations, political competition today, and not only in the world's few remaining monarchies, occurs under the shadow of the kind of violence that the Book of Samuel so revealingly details.

In mercilessly and painstakingly exposing the structural tensions and contradictions of the political project, without ever denying its necessity and centrality, our author has left us an extraordinary treasure-house of insight. The document that we have inherited is also the first of its kind in world literature. The story it tells was written in great proximity to the moment of origin of the political life in the author's own community, a moment of origin that allowed an unprecedented clarity of thought and perception. The Book of Samuel is a kind of manual for all who are touched and defined by political life, be they kings, officers or subjects. It will serve them as a luminous lens through which to read their own reality and sometimes to overcome and remedy what can potentially go so wrong in politics. As a revelation, the book is an act of witnessing. The author's witnessing assumes the following form: "The people of Israel embarked on this risky political project out of necessity. The deep problems inherent in such a project can be seen and analyzed most clearly in its initial phase. Here is my account of this experiment. Beware of what I saw and have told you now."

Notes

INTRODUCTION: THE EMERGENCE OF POLITICS

1. Without focusing on the literary qualities of the Book of Samuel, we have nevertheless benefited enormously from the works of those scholars who made this their principal concern. Meticulous readings of the literary dimensions of the book can be found in Jan P. Fokkelman's four-volume work, *Narrative Art and Poetry in the Books of Samuel* (Assen: Van Gorcum, 1981–1993). Sensitivity to the literary qualities of the book also marks the running commentary of Shimon Bar-Efrat, *1 and 2 Samuel: With Introduction and Commentary* 2 vols. (in Hebrew), (Tel Aviv: Am Oved, 1996). Robert Alter shrewdly explores the literary dimensions as well in the copious annotations to his translation of Samuel. Moshe Garsiel's book *Samuel, In the World of the Bible: 1 and 2 Samuel*, 2 vols. (in Hebrew) (Tel Aviv: Revivim, 1984, 1989), too, examines narrative techniques and structures. Yair Zackovitch's *David from Shepherd to Messiah* (in Hebrew) (Jerusalem: Ben Zvi, 1995) also concentrates on the literary qualities of the work, highlighting among other features the mirroring technique by which the author of the Book of Samuel alludes implicitly to other biblical narratives. Another interpretation of David's character and role based on a literary reading can be found in Paul Borgman, *David, Saul, & God: Rediscovering an Ancient Story* (Oxford: Oxford University Press, 2008).

Deserving special mention among many individual essays devoted to literary analyses of narrative portions of the book is Meir Sternberg, *The Poetics of Biblical Narrative: Ideological Literature and the Drama of Reading* (Bloomington: Indiana University Press, 1987), chapter 6, devoted to the narrative of the killing of Uriah. Uriel Simon has written three essays that concern the literary analysis of some of the narratives discussed below, including the narrative of "Saul in Ein-Dor" and "That Man is You" in his *Reading Prophet Narratives*, translated from Hebrew by Lenn J. Schramm (Bloomington: Indiana University Press, 1997) chapters 3 and 4; and also "Abigail Prevents David from

Spilling Blood: Political Violence in the Bible" in *Seek and Pursue Peace* (in Hebrew) (Tel Aviv: Yedihot Achronot, 2002), pp. 177–217. Simon responded to Perry and Sternberg's essay in "An Ironic Approach to a Bible Story: On the Interpretation of the Story of David and Bathsheba," *Hasifrut* 2 (1970) pp. 598–607; Shimon Bar-Efrat, *Narrative Art in the Bible* (London: Bloomsbury, 2004), pp. 239–82, devotes an extensive chapter to the Amnon and Tamar Story.

2. The question of whether the Book of Samuel had one author in the strict sense of the term is a matter of heated scholarly debate. Following Martin Noth's Deuteronomistic theory, first published in 1943, a scholarly trend emerged claiming that the book was based on pre-existing material and heavily edited by a Deuteronomistic redactor or compiler, and thus that no single coherent voice is present in the book. Instead, according to this school, an early layer has to be laboriously uncovered by stripping away the strong and essentially distorting editorial voice that was added at a later date. This argument is developed at length in two volumes by Robert Polzin, *Samuel and the Deuteronomist* (Bloomington: Indiana University Press, 1993) and *David and the Deuteronomist* (Bloomington: Indiana University Press, 1993). For an extensive and updated scholarly discussion of the debate, see the collection of essays in *Is Samuel Among the Deuteronomists?* edited by Cynthia Edenburg and Juha Pakkala (Atlanta: Society of Biblical Literature, 2013). We concur with those who argue that the Deuteronomistic impact on Samuel is negligible. Besides minor additions along the way, only two chapters (not analyzed in our book), 1 Sam 12 and 2 Sam 7, were added by a Deuteronomistic scribe. These two chapters convey the Deuteronomistic tradition both in content and style. Another addition that was later appended to the book and that is alien to the work's literary voice and concerns is 2 Sam 21–24, though this add-on, as it happens, does not belong to the Deuteronomistic tradition. Our second and third chapters deal with long narrative sequences composed, in our view, by a single author who is clearly in full command of the subject. The texts that we discuss in these two chapters belong to the unit that biblical scholars call the "Succession Narrative," which extends from 2 Sam 9 to 2 Sam 20 and also includes the first two chapters of 1 Kings. The unity and scope of the succession narrative were first analyzed and discussed by Leonhard Rost, *Die Überlieferung von der Thronnachfolge Davids* (Stuttgart: W. Kohlhammer, 1926). Rost's perspective was embraced by Gerhard von Rad, "The Beginnings of History Writing in Ancient Israel," in *The Problem of the Hexateuch and Other Essays*, translated by E. W. Tureman (New York: McGraw-Hill, 1955), pp. 166–204. An extensive monograph devoted to further analyzing the unity and aim of this long narrative section is Roger Norman Whybray, *The*

Succession Narrative: A Study of II Sam. 9–20 and I Kings 1 and 2 (Naperville: SCM Press, 1968). Their view of the unity of authorship and aim of the succession story was challenged by Shimon Bar-Efrat, "The Succession Story of David's Throne: A Renewed Examination of an Accepted Position," in *Isaac Arieh Zeligman's Book*, vol. 1, edited by Y. Zakowitch and A. Rofe (in Hebrew) (Jerusalem: Rubinshtein Press, 1983), pp. 185–211.

In our judgment, proponents of the single-authorship hypothesis are correct. As will become clear as our analysis unfolds, only unity of authorship can explain the complete command of the materials so brilliantly displayed in the succession narrative, especially starting from 2 Sam 11. In other sections of the Book of Samuel, however, especially in the sections we analyze in our first chapter, the same author was at times incorporating previous sources and small narrative units that stemmed from diverse traditions, attempting to weave them into a coherent story. This conclusion can be inferred from the various duplicates or "doublets" that appear in the story, such as the two stories of how David entered Saul's court—1 Sam 16:17–23 and 1 Sam 17:17–18:5. (The verse at 1 Sam 17:16 is a rather crude attempt at harmonizing these two sources). Other repetitions that might have their origin in different traditions recycled by our author include the three coronation stories of Saul—1 Sam 9:1–10:16, and 1 Sam 10:17–27, and 1 Sam 11:12–15. Similar retellings appear in the story of Saul's pursuit of David, which includes two attempts by Saul to kill David—1 Sam 18:10–13 and 1 Sam 19:9–10. Another example is David's twice-over refusal to kill Saul when he has the chance. The two versions of this carefully staged nonregicide seem to reflect two different traditional accounts of the same event (1 Sam 24:2–22 and 1 Sam 26:1–25). It would thus be more accurate to claim that in these passages, unlike what we find in the succession narrative, one and the same author worked with preexisting traditions and materials, plaiting them into a coherent narrative of his own. The divergence in the degree of coherence and internal consistency and flow between 2 Sam 11–20 plus I Kings 1–2 and the rest of the narrative is based on differences between the inherited stories being retold. In narrating the rise of Saul, his competition with David, his eventual demise, and the establishment of David's monarchy, our author created a relatively consistent and well-crafted, novel-like narrative. Yet because of its epic qualities, dealing as it does with the rise of two kings and the struggle between them and spanning a narrative arc that encompasses momentous historical events, this chronicle had to incorporate familiar lore that had long been widely circulating concerning Saul and David. Not including them, our author must have concluded, would have severely impugned the credibility and detracted from the acceptability of the narrative.

Rather than expurgating well-known but repetitive or contradictory characterizations and occurrences, therefore, the author did his best to weave them into a coherent whole, using them selectively to develop his characters and to explore the inner workings of power politics. Narrating David's story without mentioning, for example, that he was a gifted musician brought to Saul's court on that account, would have departed too radically from what everyone knew or thought they knew about David. In the more compact succession narrative, by contrast, the author was able to zoom in, concentrating on particular episodes that must have been relatively unencumbered by traditional storylines given their relatively narrower time scope. This enabled the author to be in much fuller command of the narrative development in 2 Sam 9–20 and 1 Kgs 1–2 than in the earlier parts of his story.

3. See for example Walter Dietrich, who develops the idea of an independent northern origin of the Samuel-Saul narrative in his book *The Early Monarchy in Israel: The Tenth Century BCE*, Translated by Joachim Vette (Atlanta: Society of Biblical Literature, 2007), pp. 174–77, 247–48, 272–74. For a "northern" source of the Saul-and-David cycle and the diverse ways in which the story has been parsed in the scholarship in relation to promonarchical and antimonarchical sentiments, see P. Kyle McCarter in his introduction to the commentary on Samuel in The Anchor Bible Series, *1 Samuel* (New York: Doubleday & Company, 1980), pp. 18–23. See also Walter Brueggemann, *David's Truth: In Israel's Imagination and Memory* (Philadelphia: Fortress Press, 1985), who argues, among other things, that the complexity of the narrative can be explained in part by an editorial decision to combine pro-David and anti-David sources. This view of two different sources and authors, one narrating David's rise to power and the other telling the story of David's reign, has become common in the scholarship. The proposed division depends on the alleged pro-David and anti-David tone of these sections, though scholars disagree on the exact identity of the passages belonging to the two supposed sources. See Jakob Grønbaek, *Die Geschichte vom Aufstieg Davids (1.Sam – 2.Sam.5): Tradition und Komposition,* (Copenhagen: Munksgaard, 1971), pp. 25–35.

   For another important and meticulous attempt at reconstructing the multiple voices allegedly audible in the text, their sequence, and their composition in relation to their political and historical aims, see Jacob L. Wright, *David, King of Israel, and Caleb in Biblical Memory* (Cambridge: Cambridge University Press, 2014). An important contribution of this book is Wright's original emphasis on political dimensions such as the role of war memorials and narratives in shaping political status and prestige.

4. Prominent examples of this approach are P. Kyle McCarter, "The Apology of David," *Journal of Biblical Literature* 99 (1980), pp. 489–504;

Baruch Halpern, *David's Secret Demons: Messiah, Murderer, Traitor, King* (Cambridge: Eerdmans, 2001); Steven L. McKenzie, *King David: A Biography* (New York: Oxford University Press, 2000); and Joel Baden, *The Historical David: The Real Life of an Invented Hero* (New York: Harper, 2013). In the innumerable commentaries on the Book of Samuel, attitudes toward the character of David run the gamut from an apologia that can never fully erase all taint, since the actual historical reality that needed to be retold and smoothed over was far worse (as argued by the authors just cited), to the claim that the book is a rather incoherent narrative reflecting David's sheer "luck" and God's arbitrary and problematic choices, including God's rejection of Saul for no real reason and his decision to embrace the lecherous and treacherous David instead. Representative of this last approach is David Gunn's *The Story of King David: Genre and Interpretation* (Sheffield, England: JSOT Press, 1978). To get a flavor of how polarized *Samuel* scholarship can be, compare Robert Polzin's *David and the Deuteronomist*, which interprets the book as a post-Exilic excoriation of monarchy aimed at revealing the extent of David's failures, with Paul Borgman's *David, Saul, & God: Rediscovering an Ancient Story*, which argues strongly for David's exemplary greatness. This dazzling array of mutually inconsistent reactions by careful readers of the Book of Samuel suggests how little can be gained from turning the quest for a partisan agenda into the centerpiece of one's investigation. A more nuanced view, rejecting attempts to distill the political purpose of the book from its literary spin, is articulated by David A. Bosworth in "Evaluating King David: Old Problems and Recent Scholarship" *Catholic Biblical Quarterly*, 68 (2006), pp. 191–210. For a rejection of both the apologetic and adversarial options, see as well Nadav Na'aman, "Saul, Benjamin and the Emergence of Biblical Israel (Part 2)," *Zeitschrift für die Alttestamentliche Wissenschaft*, 121 (2009), pp. 342–48.

5. For recent important biographies of David, see Jonathan Kirsch, *King David: The Life of the Man Who Ruled Israel* (New York: Ballantine Books, 2000), Robert Pinsky, *The Life of David* (New York: Schocken Press, 2005), and David Wolpe, *David: The Divided Heart* (New Haven: Yale Press, 2014).

6. In his book *The Hebrew Republic: Jewish Sources and the Transformation of European Political Thought* (Cambridge: Harvard University Press, 2012), Eric Nelson examines the extensive references to the Book of Samuel in early modern political thought. Joshua Berman's book *Created Equal: How the Bible Broke with Ancient Political Thought* (Oxford: Oxford University Press, 2011), is the most ambitious attempt to date to unearth the sources of modern Western political ideals in the biblical tradition.

7. Critics of our approach might argue that the Book of Samuel presents us not with a masterpiece of political theory but only with a masterful political narrative about dynastic politics in an archaic, clan-based society. Such an objection to our reading implies that we have in some way extracted a series of theoretical claims about sovereign power in general from a particular history of the Unified Monarchy that would support a variety of other ideas as well. While understanding the source and rationale of this charge, we do not find it persuasive. Our author is no mere reporter of events; he is an all-knowing narrator who adds to what would otherwise be a skeleton of historical materials a detailed and artfully constructed account stemming from his creative and fertile mind. He has carefully crafted his narrative to accentuate structural and dynamic patterns that continue to reappear throughout political life even today. As we shall see, for example, in chapter 2, dealing with the unleashing of political violence against innocent subjects, our author fashions a series of dialogues that in principle could be known only to the interlocutors. Therefore, these intimate exchanges cannot be read as a mere reporting of events. They are obviously imagined and invented by the author. Through them he subtly explores the way the very indeterminacy of the object of the ruler's paranoid suspiciousness makes it liable to manipulation and expansion, leading to irrational overkill, and how the hierarchical organization indispensable to the state-building project not only gives the ruler the capacity to act through a series of emissaries and proxies, but also offers easy deniability, encouraging the ruler to develop intentions that would never occur to agents held responsible for their actions. The author of the Book of Samuel constructs his narrative in order to bring these structural themes into high relief, among other reasons. Casting these themes in narrative form does not detract from but rather adds to their theoretical subtlety and power. It is for this reason that our reading should be understood not as an attempt to extrapolate theoretical lessons from a rich political narrative but rather as an attempt to uncover the central theoretical themes embedded by the author throughout the narrative.

8. As background to the narrative, Whybray's *The Succession Narrative* stresses the Egyptian wisdom literature that emerged and was directed to court advisers and officials. Yet the kind of prudent advice for rulers to which he helpfully draws our attention does not reach the penetrating level of the Book of Samuel's explorations of power.

9. The question of the historicity of the Samuel narratives involves two indirectly related issues. The first concerns the time of the writing of the book and the second relates to the extent to which its narratives portray historical reality. Scholars have assigned different dates for the composition of the body of the book. One opinion is that the book was written in close proximity to the events to which it refers, namely that

it was authored around the late tenth century BCE. Another opinion is that the book was composed in the late eighth century or early seventh century BCE, three hundred years later than the events it presumes to relate. Still another opinion is that it was written as late as the fifth or fourth centuries BCE. A parallel divergence marks the scholarly discussion of the second issue, the historicity of the narrative. Scholarly opinions range from (a) the maximalist view that sees the narratives as genuine sources for historical reconstruction even when not supported by other reliable evidence such as material or archeological findings, through (b) the view that indeed Saul and David existed as historical figures, even if the glorifying of David's kingship and its territorial aggrandizement has been highly inflated, implying that the Unified Monarchy is an invention that was achieved only later and that the historical David was actually a local chieftain residing in a midsize village called Jerusalem, to (c) the minimalist view that interprets the stories as completely fictional, having never been vindicated by any archeological evidence, and implying that neither Saul nor David ever existed. Naturally, the minimalist view is prevalent among scholars who date the composition of the text to the fifth or fourth century BCE. A good summary and discussion of the debate concerning the second issue appears in Israel Finkelstein and Amihai Mazar, *The Quest for the Historical Israel: Debating Archaeology and the History of Early Israel*, edited by Brian B. Schimdt (Atlanta: Society of Biblical Literature, 2007) pp. 101–39. For useful overviews of the debate concerning the time of the writing and composition of the book, see Moshe Garsiel, "The Stages of the Composition of the Book of Samuel, Its Literary Aims, and its Value as a Historical Source" (in Hebrew), *Beit Mikra* 54, 2 (2009), pp. 21–69; Moshe Garsiel, "The Book of Samuel: Its Composition, Structure, and Significance as a Historical Source," *Journal of Hebrew Scriptures* 10 (2010), pp. 2–42; and Walter Dietrich, *Die Samuelbücher im deuteronomistischen Geschichtswerk* (Stuttgart: Kohlhammer, 2012). It is tempting to plunge into these debates and stake out one position or another. But the political insights of the Book of Samuel and their structural significance, on which we will be focusing, are independent of the questions of when the book was written and to what degree it is historically accurate or entirely fictional.

10. See Baruch Halpern, *The Constitution of the Monarchy in Israel* (Chico: Scholars Press 1981).

11. For a classic formulation of the ancient Near Eastern political theology of monarchy, see Henry Frankfort, *Kingship and the Gods: A Study of Ancient Near Eastern Religion of Society and Nature* (Chicago: Chicago University Press, 1948).

12. For the standards to which kings in the ancient Near East were ostensibly made accountable, see Haim Tadmor, "Monarchy and the Elite in

Assyria and Babylonia: The Question of Royal Accountability," in *The Origins and Diversity of Axial Age Civilizations,* edited by S. N. Eisenstadt (Albany: State University of New York Press, 1986), pp. 203–324. Peter Machinist has provided an illuminating list of critical statements on the failures of kings to comply with the standards that they were expected to respect in his article "Hosea and the Ambiguity of Kingship in Ancient Israel," in *Constituting the Community Studies on the Polity of Ancient Israel, In Honor of Dean MacBride Jr,* edited by J. T. Strong and S. S. Tuel (Winona Lake.: Eisenbrauns, 2005), pp. 174–77. See as well Garry N. Knoppers, "Dissonance and Disaster in the Legend of Kitra," *Journal of the American Oriental Society* 114 (1994), pp. 572–82.

13. On the rejection of monarchy in early biblical political theology and the ideology of the Book of Judges, see Martin Buber, *Kingship of God,* translated by Richard Scheimann (New York: Harper & Row, 1967); Yehezkel Kaufmann, *The History of Israel's Faith* (in Hebrew) (Jerusalem: Bialik Press, 1965), vol. 1 pp. 686–708, vol. 2 pp. 95–99, 160–62, 371–74, 397–400; George E. Mendenhall, *The Tenth Generation: The Origins of the Biblical Period* (Baltimore: Johns Hopkins University Press, 1974), pp. 1–31.

14. "And the men of Israel saw that Abimelech had died and each man went back to his place" (Judges 9:55).

15. The concluding chapters of the Book of Judges (19–21) present a condition of radical disunity that culminated in a bitter civil war. The narrative of these three chapters, which seems to convey a sharp internal critique of the political theology of the book itself, introduces the events that led to the civil war with the verse, "In those days, when there was no king in Israel" (Judges 19:1). The narrative ends portentously with the very same formulation but emphasizing this time that the absence of monarchy spells utter anarchy: "In those days there was no king in Israel. Every man did what is right in his own eyes" (Judges 21:25). Scholars, however, debate whether this was an original section of the book or a later addition. For that debate, see Moshe Eilat, *Samuel and the Establishment of the Monarchy* (in Hebrew) (Jerusalem: Magnes Press, 1998), pp. 61–2 and footnote 20.

16. Michael Walzer, in his book *In God's Shadow: Politics in the Hebrew Bible* (New Haven: Yale University Press, 2012), argues convincingly that God's overwhelming political presence throughout biblical literature didn't allow for the carving out of a worldly space capable of supporting the emergence of autonomously human and therefore authentically political action. In light of Walzer's analysis, the Book of Samuel represents a moment of breakthrough within biblical literature precisely when God relinquished his monopoly over politics, that is, when Israel's unified and dynastic monarchy emerged.

17. Isaiah 11 and Daniel 4 provide other striking examples of the mythic political theology of kingship.

18. Moshe Eilat, *Samuel and the Establishment of the Monarchy*, pp. 57–80; and Matityahu Zevat, "The Biblical Narrative of the Establishment of the Monarchy" (in Hebrew), *Tarbiz* 36 (1967), pp. 99–109. Although, when "all the elders of Israel assembled and came to Samuel at Ramah," saying to him: "set over us a king to rule us, like all the nations" (1 Sam 8:4–5), what they went on to establish was by no means a slavish copy of neighboring political systems. Baruch Halpern stresses the singularity of the new Israelite monarchy in his important observation that this "is the only text in the ancient Near East to describe the introduction of kingship to a society as a human political decision" (*David's Secret Demons*, p. 18).

19. For this observation see Shimon Bar-Efrat's commentary (p. 127). See as well Moshe Garsiel's observations on Samuel's speech that includes, among other elements, an ominous repetition of the verb "to take," and moves from the harsher to the lighter—the taking of the sons and daughters to the seizure of property. "Samuel's Speech Concerning the Law of the King" (in Hebrew), *Thought in the Bible* 5 (1988), pp. 112–36. As another commentator suggestively remarks, "From Samuel's description one would hardly think that a national army could benefit anyone other than the king." Lyle Eslinger, *Kingship of God in Crisis. A Close Reading of 1 Samuel 1–12* (Sheffield: JSOT Press, 1985), p. 273.

CHAPTER 1: THE GRIP OF POWER

1. On 9:10, see Robert Alter's annotation to his translation (p. 48); Walter Brueggemann, *First and Second Samuel* (Louisville: John Knox Press, 1990), p. 71; and Georg Hentschel, *Saul: Schuld, Reue und Tragik eines "Gesalbten"* (Leipzig: Evangelische Verlagsanstalt, 2003), p. 41.

2. The implication that David scripted his own accession to the throne is reinforced by the story of how Saul was swept unwillingly into the kingship, following a script written wholly by others.

3. Saul's self-effacing protest of unworthiness could represent a purely conventional way to respond to an offer of an important role and title. In this case, however, given the way the lad takes the initiative in his dialogue with Saul, the humility seems genuine. In other instances where lads appear (some to be discussed below), they are consistently presented as mere pawns of the powerful. Saul's hesitant exchange with his lad is therefore a revealing exception.

4. The sequence of the three coronations is considered by some scholars to be another sign of the multiplicity of voices and sources sutured together in Samuel's text. Yet, even if these narratives derive from different traditions, in our author's hands they serve to dramatize the

historical novelty of monarchy, its origin in the popular demand for national security, the difficulties encountered in establishing it against the will of high religious authorities, and the complex relation of Saul to power, especially his palpable reluctance to seize it.

5. 1 Sam 10:8.

6. On Samuel's problematic timing and his ambiguous intentions, see Robert Polzin, *Samuel and the Deuteronomist*, pp. 129–30, and Robert Alter's notes in his commentary to Samuel 13:10 and 13:14, pp. 72–3. This potentially critical view of Samuel is supported by the narrative's effort to portray Saul's dire situation and the pressures he was under. The ambivalence towards Samuel in our text begins already at the moment when Samuel is said to have futilely hoped to ensconce his corrupt sons as his heirs. His feeling of being betrayed by the people's demand for a warrior-king pervades the entire narrative. It is noteworthy that, later on, the ghost of Samuel mentions only the failure to carry out God's commands about the Amalekites, not Saul's offering a sacrifice in Samuel's absence, to explain why God turned away from Saul (1 Sam 28:18–19).

7. Samuel might have prophetic insight into the future election of Saul's substitute, as David Kimchi, the medieval interpreter of the late twelfth and early thirteenth century from Provence, claims; but Samuel's prophetic gifts, if they are being exercised here, do not account for the fact that the prophet used the past tense, emphasizing that Saul's successor has already been elected.

8. To be sure, since Saul was bringing the best of the livestock to Gilgal to sacrifice at God's temple (and may even have been bringing Agag there for execution), he cannot reasonably be condemned for intending to use the booty for basely human purposes. This line of argument, assuming that Saul is being punished disproportionately for the breach of a cultic technicality, is developed in David M. Gunn, *The Fate of King Saul* (Sheffield: JSOT Press, 1980), pp. 41–56. For the seeming triviality of the sins for which Saul's dynasty was forever cut off, also see J. Alberto Soggin, *Introduzione all'Antico Testamento* (Brescia: Paideia, 1968), pp. 250–51.

9. For some speculations for the meaning of Samuel's grief over Saul, see Alter's note on p. 94; Walter Brueggemen, *First and Second Samuel* (Louisville, John Know Press, 1990), p. 117; Georg Hentschel, *Saul. Schuld, Reue und Tragik eines "Gesalbten"* (Leipzig: Evangelische Verlagsanstalt, 2003), p. 97.

10. Troubled by that paradox, David Kimchi argued that God's commitment not to regret his promise was now channeled into the promise he made to David to become the king. In his commentary, *Mezudat David,* the seventeenth-century David Altshuler claimed that God never promised Saul an everlasting dynasty. See as well Isaac

Abravanel, *Commentary on the Early Prophets* (Jerusalem: Torah ve'Da'at, 1956), p. 241. On this point, see Bar-Efrat's commentary, pp.195–96. For another intriguing approach to this question see Yairah Amit, "'The Glory of Israel Does Not Deceive or Change His Mind': On the Reliability of Narrator and Speakers in Biblical Narrative," *Prooftexts* 12 3 (1992) 1, pp. 201–12.

11. God rebukes Samuel for his mistake in assuming that the oldest son, Eliab, should be king, an assumption that Samuel voiced when Eliab was first presented to him: "Ah yes! Before the LORD stands His anointed." And the LORD said to Samuel, "Look not to his appearance and to his lofty stature, for I have cast him aside. For not as man sees does God see. For man sees with the eyes and the LORD sees with heart" (1 Sam 16:6–7). This rebuke (as was noticed already by the Midrash, Yalkut Shimony on Samuel, 108) is related to the presumed power of Samuel as a "seer." The critical attitude toward Samuel conveyed in this section, as in other sections as well, casts doubt on the claim that our author is making a partisan case for the prophetic point of view. The debatable theory that the prophetic northern viewpoint is dominant in the redaction and rendering of the book is adopted by P. Kyle McCarter throughout his Anchor Bible commentary on the Book of Samuel.

12. David's political ambition is powerfully portrayed in the narrative, especially in passages where his attempts to conceal it are nonjudgmentally disclosed. Sent by his father, David arrived at the front in order to bring provisions to his older brothers who were serving in Saul's army. Just as he came onto the battlefield with the provisions, Goliath sallied forth to challenge the Israelites while mocking their God. This information is immediately followed by some remarkable verses containing the first statement uttered by David in the book: "And a man of Israel said, 'Have you seen this man coming up? Why, to insult Israel he comes up! And the man who strikes him down the king will enrich with a great fortune, and his daughter he will give him, and his father's household he will make free of levies in Israel.' And David said to the men who were standing with him, 'What will be done for the man who strikes down yonder Philistine and takes away insult from Israel? For who is this uncircumcised Philistine that he should insult the battle lines of the living God?' And the troops said to him to the same effect, 'Thus will be done for the man who strikes him down'" (1 Sam 17:25–27). David was making sure that the coveted prize had indeed been promised; and, as Alter notes, he concealed his desire for reward and glory with an expression of pious outrage at the religious desecration involved in Goliath's challenge. He was moved to confront the formidable warrior not for personal ambition alone, in other words, but to redeem the honor of Israel and Israel's God. Upon hearing of David's inquiry into

the reward for accepting Goliath's dare and his boastful proposal to take matters into his own hands, his older brother scolds him: "And Eliab his oldest brother heard when he spoke with the men, and Eliab was incensed with David and he said, 'Why is it you have come down, and with whom have you left that bit of flock in the wilderness? I'm the one who knows your impudence and your wicked impulses, for it's to see the battle that you've come.' And David said, 'What now have I done? It was only talk.' And he turned away from him toward someone else, and he spoke to the same effect, and the troops answered him with words like the ones before" (1 Sam 17:28–30). David's main characteristics, his ambition, his peculiar genius at mixing mundane political motives with high moral and religious goals, his evasiveness, and his confidence and determination are all beautifully presented in the very first words he speaks as a character in the narrative.

13. See Alter's comment on 1 Sam 18:20, p. 115.

14. On the nature of David's inscrutable inner life as thoroughly political, and its stark contrast to Saul's transparent state, see Robert Alter, *The Art of Biblical Narrative* (second edition) (New York: Basic Books, 2011), pp. 143–52. The striking contrast between David's inscrutable opaqueness and the vulnerable exposure of Saul and his family is emphasized as well by Polzin, *Samuel and the Deuteronomist*, p. 178.

15. In a later stage of the narrative when David becomes the king of Judah and makes a pact with Abner, the commander of Saul's heir's army, to gain control over all of Israel, he demands as a prior condition that he get back Michal who had been taken from him when Saul began to pursue him. In the interim, Michal had been wed to another man. The author of Samuel left us a wonderfully illuminating scene of the forced return of Michal to David, revealing the stark difference between the loving innocence of her then-husband and the politically calculating and amoral disposition of men in power: "And Abner sent messengers to David in his stead, saying, 'To whom should the land belong? Make a pact with me and, look, my hand will be with you to bring round to you all Israel.' And he said, 'Good. I shall make a pact with you. But one thing do I ask of you, namely, you shall not see my face until you bring Michal daughter of Saul when you come to see my face.' And David sent messengers to Ish-bosheth son of Saul, saying, 'Give back my wife, Michal, whom I betrothed with a hundred Philistine foreskins.' And Ish-bosheth sent and took her from her husband, from Paltiel son of Laish. And her husband went with her, weeping as he went after her, as far as Bahurim. And Abner said to him, 'Go back!' And he went back" (2 Sam 3:12–16). As Alter notes in his commentary, Paltiel's moving and innocent weeping, trailing mournfully after his wife as she is taken from him by force majeure and being harshly driven away by Abner, contrasts vividly with the calculatingly political attitudes of David and

Saul, neither of whom hesitate to instrumentalize Michal as a pawn in their contest for power. (See Alter's note, p. 211.) At this point David is no longer merely trying to marry into a politically prominent family, which is a nearly universal way of treating women instrumentally in most societies prior to the nineteenth century. Instead, he wants Michal to remain childless so that the Saulide line will expire. Thus, like Saul in the earlier episode, David is here violating a love-bond to eliminate a potential rival to the throne. That is the kind of instrumentalization that deserved to be called cynical, callous, and morally odious.

16. As suggested in note 15 to chapter 1, rulers throughout much of history, and in many societies even today, treat daughters instrumentally, as when Talmai king of Geshur gave his daughter Maacha (mother of Absalom) in marriage to David in order to secure a strategic alliance (2 Sam 3:3–4). This common practice certainly provides a revealing window onto the unsentimental ploys of status-seeking and status-defending families throughout history. But the way Saul instrumentalized Michal's love for David and the way David trampled on the Michal-Paltiel relation have an altogether different and less morally palatable character. After detailing how the single-minded desire to obtain or retain power can corrupt parental love for daughters, moreover, our author goes on to explore the flip side, that is, how overly indulgent parental love for sons can corrupt and corrode the wise exercise of sovereign power. On this mesmerizing and disorienting effect of paternal sentimentalism on the otherwise calculating exercise of supreme authority, see our chapter 3 below.

17. In order to highlight the differences between Saul and David, the narrative presents them both as being initially dispatched on errands by their fathers. Having been sent by his father to retrieve the stray asses, Saul wished to return home, while David, sent by his father to carry provisions to his brothers, shrewdly and energetically exploited the opportunity, throwing himself into the fight with Goliath and earning thereby a place at court, far away from home.

18. The medieval commentators, following the Aramaic Targum, interpret "he prophesied" as meaning he became mad or incoherent ("vay-ishtatei") and, following Rashi, they claim that the analogy makes sense because the words of the prophet and the words of the madman might both be mysterious. See Rashi's commentary to 1 Sam 18:10.

19. David's lie is exacerbated by the fact that, while concealing his fugitive status, he adopted a tone of imperative command when addressing Ahimelech. On David's language see Bar-Efrat's commentary on verse 4, p. 271, and Alter's commentary on verse 10, p. 133.

20. Mishnah Berachot, 9, 6.

21. As several commentators have noted, the tearing of the skirt of Saul's cloak echoes the moment when Saul grasped and tore the skirt of

Samuel's cloak, an act taken by Samuel as a symbol of God's tearing the kingdom from Saul (1 Sam 15:27–29). The parallel suggests that David, by this rough gesture, dramatized the transfer of the monarchy from Saul to himself.

22. See Polzin, *Samuel and the Deuteronomist*, p. 210, and Alter's annotation to verse 7, p. 148.

23. The publicly staged demonstration of innocence appears as well in the parallel story narrated in chapter 26. The similarities between these stories have convinced scholars that this is the same story told twice, though some subtle differences are worth noting. On the differences see Bar-Efrat, 1 Samuel (pp. 327–28).

24. On the possible interpretation of the differences between the account given by the Amalekite of Saul's death and the way it was described and narrated, see Yaira Amit, "The Death of Saul Three Variations" (in Hebrew), *Beit Mikra* 100 (1985), pp. 92–102.

25. In such cases, the text forces its readers to imagine counterfactual options, and indeed medieval commentators argue about what David would have done had he not been excused from the battle. Ralbag, the fourteenth-century Provençal commentator Levi ben Gershon, makes the claim that David would have intervened on the side of Saul's forces, while Abravanel interestingly refuses to accept such a contention, arguing in emphatic terms that joining the Israelite side would have been a betrayal of his pact with Achish and therefore unworthy of David. If David had participated in the battle, according to Abravanel, he would have played the role of Achish's bodyguard, only protecting his lord while refraining from attacking the Israelites. See Abravanel, 1 Sam 29:5, p. 301.

26. See Alter's comment to 1 Sam 30:1, p. 183. Polzin raises the interesting point that David, in this very chapter, after his raid in the desert, instituted the rule that soldiers who remain in the rear with the gear deserve the same share in the spoils of war as soldiers at the front (1 Sam 30:23–24). Remaining at the rear of Achish's army, therefore, David, following his own ruling, shared with the Philistines at the front responsibility for Saul's defeat. See Polzin, *Samuel and the Deuteronomist*, p. 223. It is noteworthy as well that the narrative (1 Sam 30:26–31) makes a point of telling us that when Saul was defeated and David was raiding the south, David sent the spoils of his incursions to the elders of Judah, thus garnering their support and preparing the ground for his own coronation as king of Judah immediately after the defeat and death of Saul.

27. The possibility that the death of Abner, who had made himself strong in the House of Saul, while potentially dangerous for David, may also have served to consolidate David's grip over all of Israel is raised by

H. W. Herzberg, *I & II Samuel* (London: SCM Press, 1964), p. 261, among other commentators.

28. For an incisive analysis of David's ambivalent "favor," see Leo G. Perdue, "Is there anyone left of the house of Saul . . . ?" *Journal for the Study of the Old Testament* 30 (1984), pp. 67–84. In Absalom's rebellion David indeed suspected Mephibosheth of conspiring against him (2 Sam 16:1–4 and 19:25–29). When David was forced to flee from Jerusalem, Mephibosheth stayed out of David's sight and didn't join David in his temporary exile. Mephibosheth's absence was what first triggered David's suspicions (2 Sam, 16:3; 19:26). At a later stage of the narrative (2 Sam 21:1–14) we are told that David handed over seven of Saul's descendants to the Gibeonites to be executed by them as retribution for Saul's breaking the covenant that he had made with them. This passage provides the most powerful evidence for David's drive to eradicate the rival dynasty's male line. We haven't cited this part of the story in building our case for David's instrumental treatment of the deaths of innocent subjects, however, since it seems that the chapter that recounts these events is an appendix that was not part of the original narrative.

29. On the nature of David's inscrutable inner life as thoroughly political, and its stark contrast to Saul's transparent state, see note 14 in chapter 1.

30. Abigail's appeal to David's political self-interest was captured by a passage in the Talmud that constructed the dialogue between Abigail and David in the following manner: "'To have shed blood,' you are going to become the king of Israel and it will be said about you that you are a murderer (one who sheds blood)" (Jerusalem Talmud, Sanhedrin 2, 3). See also Uriel Simon, "Abigail Prevents David from Spilling Blood: Political Violence in the Bible," in *Seek and Pursue Peace* (in Hebrew) (Tel Aviv: Yedihot Achronot, 2002), pp. 213–14. On the possible political advantage gained by David's eventual marriage to Abigail see Jon Levinson, "1 Samuel 25 as Literature and Politics," *The Catholic Biblical Quarterly* 40 (1978), pp. 24–8.

31. See footnote 15 to chapter 1 above describing the loving attachment of the anonymous figure Paltiel ben Laish to Michal in contrast with her coldhearted instrumentalization by David and Saul.

32. Our text doesn't reveal how the ghostwife recognized Saul; see Moshe Garsiel's discussion and suggestion in "King Saul in his Distress: Between Samuel the Prophet and the Ghostwife" (in Hebrew), *Studies in Bible and Interpretation* 6 (2002), pp. 37–8.

33. Saul asked the ghostwife to describe her vision, and from her answer it was clear to him that this was indeed Samuel: "And she said, 'An old man rises up, and he is wrapped in a cloak'" (18:14). It might have been the cloak that conveyed Samuel's presence to Saul. The cloak or

robe stands as a constant feature in the narrative of the life of Saul and Samuel and their relationship. On this point, see Polzin, *Samuel and the Deuteronomist*, pp. 218–19.

34. On the contrast between the mercilessness of Samuel the prophet and the compassion of the ghostwife, see Uriel Simon, "Saul at En-Dor: The Narrative Balance between a Pitiless Prophet and a Compassionate Witch," in *Reading Prophetic Narratives*, translated by Lenn J. Schramm (Bloomington: Indiana University Press, 1997) pp. 73–92. On the compassionate nature of the ghostwife see also Jan P. Fokkelmann, *Narrative Art and Poetry in the Books of Samuel, The Crossing Fates*, vol. 2 (Assen/Massstricht: Van Gorcum, 1986), pp. 619–22. W.A.M. Beuken flatly denies the moral heroism of the woman of Endor, arguing (unpersuasively we believe) that the author of the Book of Samuel would never have portrayed an act of human kindness being shown to one whom God had solemnly rejected. "I Samuel 28: The Prophet as 'Hammer of Witches'," *Journal for the Study of the Old Testament* 6 (1978), pp. 3–17.

CHAPTER 2: TWO FACES OF POLITICAL VIOLENCE

1. We depart here from Alter's translation, which formulates the statement as a question.

2. To emphasize Saul's state of acute paranoia, the narrator has him claim that David had made promises that only a monarch could deliver, such as appointing loyalists to military command and allocating fields seized from defeated enemies. In Saul's anxiety-ridden state, David seems to be distributing in advance the expected spoils of his conspiracy to usurp the throne.

3. As Fokkelman remarks (vol. 2, pp. 381–84), Saul repeats the term "*every one of you*" (*kulkhem*) in addressing his inner circle three times within the two verses 7 and 8, and he juxtaposes that expression with the phrase "*and none of you* was troubled for my sake" that also appears in verse 8. The contrast between "every one of you" and "none of you" is a powerful expression of Saul's paranoia and self-pity, insulating and isolating Saul as one against all.

4. 1 Sam 18:10–12; 19:9–10.

5. On verse 13, see Rashi, who interprets the accusation of oracular support as implying a relationship of subordination to a king; on the same verse, see also Kimchi's remark that the accusation assumes oracular assistance in abetting David's escape.

6. The summoning of Ahimelech is couched in official language by the formal description of Ahimelech as "Ahimelech the son of Ahitub." As Fokkelman notes in vol. 2, p. 394, Saul has swiftly moved from

plaintiff to judge, a change of roles that taints the investigation, turning it into a drumhead trial where the priest has zero chances of acquittal.

7. To underscore the priest's unquestioning assumption of David's loyalty to the crown, the narrator makes Ahimelech the only one in the dialogue up to this point who refers to David by name. Saul calls him derogatorily "the son of Jesse," as does Doeg, or "my slave" when accusing him of colluding with Jonathan, who is called "my son" rather than Jonathan. In shifting in verse 8 from "the son of Jesse" to "my slave," Saul expresses his sense of being betrayed by conspirators. Although Jonathan and David owe him allegiance due to their relationship to him—one is his son and the other his slave—both have colluded secretly against him.

8. Here we follow Bar-Efrat (p. 286–87) and Alter (p. 138) in interpreting verse 15 as a denial on Ahimelech's part, in contrast to others, among them the medieval commentators Rashi and Kimchi.

9. The existence of an inviolable boundary protected by a sense of sacredness is conveyed by the decision of the bodyguards to disobey Saul's command to execute the priests of Nob in especially striking terms. The bodyguards, we are told, "did not want to reach out their hand to stab the priests of the LORD" (1 Sam 22:17), while Saul's command was "Turn round and put to death the priests of the LORD" (1 Sam 22:17). The expression "reach out their hand" signifies a deeper unwillingness and it reminds us of David's own refusal, pronouncing the same words, to commit a sacrilegious act by killing Saul, God's anointed. The bodyguards' refusal to "reach out their hand" is also used to cast doubt on Saul's claim, in the same verse, concerning the priests: "for their hand, too, is with David" (1 Sam 22:17).

10. This example of Saul's inability to coerce his armed enforcers should be compared with the earlier episode when Saul condemned Jonathan to death for having violated the oath, of which he knew nothing, to forsake all food during the day of battle. In the end, "the troops saved Jonathan, and he did not die" (1 Sam 14:45–46).

11. David's decision to keep away from the battlefield might conceivably be justified by analogy to what we are told in a later passage, where, after Abishai saved David from certain death in combat, his servants swore an oath that the monarch must never more be allowed to expose himself so rashly and must therefore never be allowed to lead them in war again, lest his death "snuff out the lamp of Israel" (2 Sam 21:17).

12. The verb "to send" appears eleven times in the narrative.

13. The opening verse, "And it happened at the turn of the year, at the time the kings sally forth," has a textual variant which substitutes "messengers" for "kings." This variant reading has developed because of the

similarity between "melakhim," which means kings, and "mala'akhim," which means messengers. There is a good reason to assume that the variant might point to a duality consciously implanted by the author, as Polzin has noted (*David and the Deuteronomist*, pp. 109–11). The variant "kings" establishes a contrast with the behavior of David who conspicuously did not sally forth, while the variant "messengers" resonates with the rest of the story, which foregrounds the pivotal role of messengers and sending.

14. In the Hebrew, David's triple question, "How Joab fared and how the troops fared and how the fighting fared," is emphasized by the term "li-shlom," which could be literally translated as "the peace of." Our author uses this sequential, cumulative inquiry into the fortune ("peace") of different subjects and the war itself to emphasize David's calculated attempt to craft an alibi to explain his summoning of Uriah. It also highlights the gap between David's pretended care for the well-being of his troops and his self-serving betrayal of Uriah. On this point, see Bar-Efrat, *2 Samuel*, p. 111. It is also worth noting that Uriah's answer is not reported. This suggests, but doesn't prove, that the king has no real interest in an answer and that his questions were in fact disingenuous.

15. The disparity between David's treachery and Uriah's fidelity is accentuated by the use of the same verb "va-yishkav" ("lay"), for David's having sexual intercourse with Bathsheba, "he lay with her" (verse 4), and for Uriah going to sleep with the servants, "And Uriah lay at the entrance of the king's house" (verse 9).

16. Meir Sternberg has raised the issue of Uriah's possible knowledge and David's possible awareness of Uriah's knowledge as an intentional gap meant to be filled by the reader in different directions. See Meir Sternberg, *The Poetics of Biblical Narrative: Ideological Literature and the Drama of Reading* (Bloomington: Indiana University Press, 1987), pp. 201-12. Responding to Sternberg's essay, Uriel Simon makes a powerful and plausible argument that no such gap actually exists in the narrative, and that Uriah was, beyond question, a loyal and innocent soldier manipulated by the king. "An Ironic Approach to a Bible Story: On the Interpretation of the Story of David and Bathsheba" (in Hebrew) *Hasifrut* 2 (1970), pp. 598–607.

17. Uriah is described by Abravanel in the following manner: "and it was because of Uriah's virtuousness that he didn't open the letter and didn't read what was in it and handed it to Joab" (2 Sam 11:11, p. 342).

18. The indirect and deniable use of the enemy to kill a rival is reminiscent of Saul's attempt to kill David via the Philistines in 1 Sam 18:25–26.

19. The Talmud suggests a difference between the servants of Saul, who refused to perform Saul's illegitimate command to kill the priests of Nob (analyzed in the first section of this chapter), and Joab's obedience

to David. From the Talmud's perspective, Saul's subordinates had the courage to refuse Saul's direct, face-to-face command, while Joab implicitly followed instructions written to him in a letter. "They (Saul" servants) were (commanded) by mouth and didn't follow, and he (Joab) was commanded by letter and he followed" (Babylonian Talmud, Sanhedrin 49a). In the Talmud's account, the contrast between conscientious objection and unreflective obedience, portrayed in these two narratives, reflects the way our author explores two very different structures of political violence.

20. The gap between David's command and Joab's performance is analyzed in Sternberg's essay, pp. 213–14.

21. Sternberg (pp. 214–18) offers another interpretation of Joab's peculiar way of telling the news to the king, ascribing to Joab the desire to tease David and play with his emotions. Alter, more attuned to the political nature of this narrative, makes the argument that Joab's attempt to micromanage the messenger's report was a matter of political calculation: "Might this, too, be calculated, as an oblique dissemination of David's complicity in Uriah's death, perhaps to be used at some future point by Joab against the king?" (Alter's commentary on verse 21, p. 255).

22. Throughout the chapter, the author avoids any condemnation or negative evaluation of David's actions. The story is recounted in a matter-of-fact rhythm and powerful tone of amoral neutrality that reflects, in the very style of writing, the benumbed dissociation of actor from action that David himself connived to impart. It is only in the last verse that the narrator discloses that David's actions were evil in the eyes of God. The delayed delivery of this negative evaluation and the subsequent punishment makes it seem at first that all is well and that the king's plot has succeeded in masking his crime through a chain of delegated actors. David married Bathsheba and the child was born and then, only after some time has passed, the moral reckoning begins, piercing retrospectively through multiple veils of dissociation and concealment.

23. Bar-Efrat points to the parallel usages of the sword in both David's message to Joab "for the sword devours sometimes one way and sometimes another" and Nathan's prophecy "the sword shall not swerve from your house evermore." See his commentary on 2 Sam 12:10, p. 121.

CHAPTER 3: DYNASTY AND RUPTURE

1. For the widely recycled contrary view that all political misfortune in the Book of Samuel can be explained solely and exclusively as divinely orchestrated retaliation for disobedience to God's commands, see, for

example, R.P. Gordon, *1 & 2 Samuel* (Sheffield: JSOT Press, 1984), p. 10.

2. The order in which David's sons were born is detailed in 2 Sam 3:2–5. Although he was chronologically number ten among David's seventeen surviving sons, Solomon was the one who eventually inherited the throne. For a discussion of why, after Amnon, Absalom, and Adonijah were killed, the other six potential heirs were bypassed in Solomon's favor, see Walter Dietrich, *David. Der Herrscher mit der Harfe* (Leipzig: Evangelische Verlagsanstalt, 2006), p. 180ff.

3. Absalom descended from a royal family on his mother's side as well, setting him apart from the rest of David's sons and providing yet another motive for his impatiently aspiring to the throne.

4. The degree to which, at this stage of biblical literature, the incest taboo applied to brother and sister from a common father but with different mothers is contested among scholars. Some scholars claim that, even though biblical law explicitly prohibited such relations (Leviticus 20:17, Deuteronomy 27:22), our narrative might reflect earlier legal norms according to which half-sibling marriages were not considered incestuous. This is the opinion of Shimon Bar-Efrat, *Narrative Art in the Bible* translated by Dorothea Shefer-Vanson (Sheffield: Sheffield Academic Press, 1987), pp. 239–40. Some evidence for this point of view is provided by Tamar's appeal to Amnon later in the narrative: "And so, speak, pray, to the king, for he will not withhold me from you" (13:13). The Talmud finds another way to circumvent a possible incest taboo (Babylonian Talmud, Sanhedrin 21a). Other interpreters assume that Tamar's plea was merely an attempt to gain time to avoid the rape.

5. In the Talmud, Jonadab is described as "wise in evildoing" (Sanhedrin 21a); see as well Rashi's comment on verse 13:3.

6. The inappropriateness of Amnon's pining away in listless depression is stressed by Jonadab's decision to address him not by name but as "ben ha-melekh" (the son of the king) in verse 4.

7. Without denying the possibility that Jonadab scripted a clash between Amnon and Absalom from personal resentment, Joel Rosenberg correctly notes that "Jonadab's motives are allowed to lie shrouded in innuendo." Among other interesting readings, he mentions the suggestion in 2 Sam 13:32–33 that Jonadab was acting as Absalom's secret agent all along, tempting Amnon into a rape which would justify a revenge killing and the elimination of Absalom's chief rival to the throne. Joel Rosenberg, *King and Kin. Political Allegory in the Hebrew Bible* (Bloomington: Indiana University Press, 1986), pp. 141–42, 157–58.

8. See the use of the verb "le-labev" in Song of Songs 4:9. On this disguised sexual reference, see Yair Zakowitch, *David: From Shepherd*

to Messiah, (in Hebrew) (Jerusalem: Ben Zvi Press, 1995), p. 86, and Kyle McCarter, *The Anchor Bible, II Samuel*, p. 322.

9. In his extended literary analysis of this chapter, Bar-Efrat points out that David's request/order to Tamar is phrased differently than Amnon's request to David (*Narrative Art in the Bible*, pp. 254–55). Amnon asked for the food to be prepared "before my eyes, that I may take nourishment from her hand" (2 Sam 13:7). In issuing his command, David omitted the personally suggestive elements, instructing Tamar as follows: "Go, pray, to the house of Amnon your brother, and prepare nourishment for him" (2 Sam 13:7–8). In David's version, Tamar was sent to the "house of Amnon," not to Amnon. This paternal rephrasing of the son's request is a subtly crafted way of disclosing how David reassures himself, almost self-deceptively, by eliding Amnon's more revealing language.

10. See Deuteronomy 22:25. On rape and sexual offenses in biblical and ancient Near Eastern laws, see Samuel Greengus, *Laws in the Bible and in Early Rabbinic Collections: The Legal Legacy of the Ancient Near East* (Eugene: Cascade books, 2011), pp. 60–70, esp. pp. 63–66. On our passage in particular, consider Tikva Frymer-Kensky, *Reading the Women of the Bible* (New York: Schocken Books, 2002), pp. 165–66.

11. Deuteronomy 22:28–29; cf. Greengus, *Laws in the Bible and in Early Rabbinic Collections*, pp. 63–68.

12. Another possible translation for "zot" could have been "that one." As Kyle McCarter notes (p. 325), Amnon's order to send Tamar "away from me" has a stronger nuance of contempt in the Hebrew term "mea'lay," as if Tamar is a burden to be removed. Bar-Efrat (*Narrative Art in the Bible*, pp. 268–69) points as well to two other features that magnify the contempt expressed in Amnon's order. One is the added term "hachutza" (outside) and the other is the powerful verb "ne'ol" (to bolt), suggesting that Tamar will keep trying to get in, so that it is not enough to send her out or merely close the door. Consider also Frymer-Kensky, *Reading the Women of the Bible*, p. 164: "Amnon does not say 'woman'; he says, 'that.' He has totally dehumanized her."

13. Isaac Abravanel, given his own personal direct and tragic experience with politics, was an astute political reader of the Book of Samuel. In his commentary he makes the point that Absalom's killing of Amnon was motivated as well by political calculations, interpreting David's future resentment of Absalom in the following way: "David thought in his heart that Absalom wasn't awakened to kill Amnon his brother solely because of Tamar, but rather, as well, because Amnon was his older brother and the lawful heir. Absalom killed Amnon to prevent him from becoming the future king inheriting his father's throne, so

that he can become the king" (2 Sam 15:1, p. 360). Central to our reading of Samuel is the way the presumably sacred and nonstrategic duty of revenge is repeatedly exploited for purposes of political expediency, as with Joab's killing of Abner, discussed above in chapter 1, and the dying David's instruction to Solomon to have Joab himself put to death, allegedly in retribution for Joab's murders of Abner and Amasa, discussed in the Conclusion.

14. Some scholars, including Kyle McCarter, are of the opinion that, even though the Masoretic text doesn't have the clause "because he loved him since he was his firstborn," the clause is an integral part of the text as it appears in the Septuagint and the manuscript variant from Qumran, and that it was deleted in the Masoretic text by a scribal error of skipping a line. See McCarter's note (pp. 319–20). Alter's counterargument in his commentary on verse 21 (p. 271) seems plausible to us.

15. Absalom's strategy for convincing his father was perceptively captured by Ralbag in his commentary to 2 Sam 13:24: "And it was preplanned by Absalom to ask the king that he should come with his servants to eat and drink and celebrate with him, knowing that this will be an unaccepted (invitation) and the king will not agree to that, but Absalom made the offer so the king will agree in the end to send Amnon, and he will not be attentive to Absalom's hatred of Amnon for what he did to his sister Tamar."

16. On David's inchoate suspicions, see Bar-Efrat's commentary to 2 Sam 13:26, p. 141.

17. It is also difficult to resist the following thought, even though it grazes the shores of speculation. In telling David that only Amnon was killed, and casually revealing his own awareness that the assassination plot had been brewing since the day of Tamar's rape, Jonadab, besides consoling the king, may also be pouring salt on his wounds. The king must have thought the following: "If Jonadab was fully aware of this danger from the day Amnon raped his sister Tamar, how could it have eluded me? And how could I have sent Amnon to expose himself unprotected to Absalom's wrath? I knew of Amnon's crime, and I was incensed by it. I wondered aloud why Absalom was insisting on Amnon's coming to his wool-shearing festivity and I was therefore, in effect, an accomplice in Amnon murder. Jonadab's seemingly innocent expressions of comfort, in other words, had a sharp edge. In comforting David, he may have actually wished to grieve him inconsolably.

18. Another brilliant case, revealing our author's awareness of the information-deficit that afflicts all rulers, appears in the later narrative of David's flight from Jerusalem after Absalom's rebellion. On his way out of the city, David was followed by Ziba who had been the

servant of Mephibosheth, Jonathan's crippled son. As we discussed in chapter 1, Mephibosheth, the last remnant of the Saulide family, was summoned to sit at David's table in Jerusalem. Wanting to show his utter loyalty to David, Ziba brought with him a large quantity of supplies to help David and his men to survive their exile from the city. Mephibosheth, on the other hand, had stayed in Jerusalem. Suspicious of Mephibosheth's absence, David asked Ziba the whereabouts of his master. At this point, Ziba misinformed David: "Why, he [Mephibosheth] is staying in Jerusalem, for he has said, 'Today the house of Israel will give back to me my father's kingdom.'" (2 Sam 16:3). This was a lie, but Ziba's calculated disinformation was brilliantly self-serving. It succeeded by playing on David's fears and suspicion of the possible revolt of the Saulide faction. Immediately upon hearing from Ziba that Mephibosheth was supposedly conspiring against him, David issued the following order: "And the king said to Ziba, 'Look, everything of Mephibosheth's is yours!'" (2 Sam 16:4). The ruler is a magnet for such lies precisely because of the great power he wields, including the capacity to transfer ownership of land by fiat. Being isolated at the top of the hierarchy, out of touch with the realities on the ground, and always depending on mediators, moreover, the ruler is acutely vulnerable to being manipulated by artfully dosed disinformation.

After the rebellion had failed, Mephibosheth denied the charges against him, claiming that Ziba intentionally abandoned him in Jerusalem, exploiting his crippled and immobile condition. David may have believed him, may have been unwilling to admit to being fooled by Ziba, or may have been unable to make up his mind about what actually had happened. In any case, he ended up making an incoherent decision, ordering the property split between Mephibosheth and Ziba rather than restoring it all to Mephibosheth (2 Sam 19:30). This is yet another precious moment in our author's uncannily subtle grasp of political realities. For another such possible case of manipulating the sovereign by feeding him disinformation, see below note 4 of chapter 4.

19. See, for example, Zakowitch's fine analysis of the echo of the sexual assault on Joseph by Potiphar's wife (Genesis 39) in the narrative of the rape of Tamar in *David: From Shepherd to Messiah*, pp. 87–9, as well as Polzin's astute analysis of the echoes of the rape of the concubine in Gibeah that led to the civil war in the last chapters of the Book of Judges, in *David and the Deuteronomist,* pp. 136–39.

20. Kimchi in his commentary drew attention perceptively to the mixed motives of the family: "The family members aim to annihilate my husband's remnant and destroy the heir so they will inherit my husband's property" (2 Sam 14:7). As mentioned above, the theme of mixed

motives is ubiquitous in the Book of Samuel, also recurring, for example, in Absalom's multiple overlapping reasons for avenging the rape
of Tamar.

21. The continuous pressure exerted by the wise woman, unsatisfied by
the king's verbal commitments, is emphasized by Bar-Efrat in his commentary, 2 Sam 14:10 (p. 150).

22. It seems that the conventional punishment for a murder within the
family was exile; such was the case with Cain, who was condemned
to permanent exile and homelessness for the murder of his brother.
The break with this norm is emphasized in the wise woman's lament
that her clan seeks the death of her surviving son, accused of fratricide. The logical implication that excessive punishments for fratricide
should be alleviated by royal decree—the central message of Joab's
script—is strengthened by an allusion to the Cain and Abel narrative
in the widow's description of the murder as occurring in the field:
"and they quarreled in the field, and there was no one to part them,
and one struck down the other and caused his death" (2 Sam 14:6),
echoing Genesis 4:8. As Kyle McCarter notes in his comment to this
section (p. 351), the wise woman framed the story so that the brother
may have acted from self-defense in a spontaneous quarrel and thus
may not have been guilty of murder after all. By recounting her sham
case in such a manner, she maneuvered the king into granting royal
protection to a purported fratricidal killer, a decree that also seemed
applicable to Absalom's fratricide, which was nevertheless essentially
different since the latter had been a planned, premeditated, and public
killing.

23. Alter p. 282; see also Bar-Efrat who notes the fatefully cold and formal
manner of this reconciliation in his annotation to 2 Sam 14:33, p. 156.

24. Absalom's chariot with horses and fifty men running before him re-
calls one of the characteristics of kingship against which Samuel in-
veighed in his memorable antimonarchical harangue: "Your sons he
will take and set for himself in his chariots and in his cavalry, and some
will run before his chariots" (1 Sam 8:11).

25. Particularly striking is the way Absalom exploits the popular grievance: "You have no one to listen to you from the king." Because being
ignored is a permanent experience of individual subjects facing the
impersonal political machine, Absalom can project a false "personal"
touch by addressing aggrieved individuals outside official alienating
structures. See Alter's note to 15:3, p. 283. McCarter makes the nice
point that Absalom is especially alive to this kind of popular resentment because of his own recent experience of being shunned by the
"unresponsive and inaccessible" king (II Samuel, p. 357).

26. At least a third of David's forces consisted of Philistine mercenaries
led by Ittai the Gittite, and including as well the palace guard, made

up of Cherethites and Pelethites. When David fled Jerusalem, they joined him in his escape, even though David, testing their loyalty, suggested that they stay in the city: "For you are a foreigner, and you are also in exile from your own place. Just yesterday you came, and today should I make you wander with us . . . Turn back, and bring back your brothers" (2 Sam 15:20). Responding with the ultimate expression of loyalty, Ittai said, "As the LORD lives, and as my lord the king lives, whatever place that my lord the king may be, whether for death or for life, there your servant will be" (2 Sam 15:21). Thus, David was saved by, among other factors, personally loyal foreign forces led by an officer from Gath, a Philistine city-state in whose army David had once served as a mercenary leader. Alexander Rofe has pointed to the heavy reliance on foreigners in David's standing military and bureaucracy as the principal reason for Absalom's widespread support both among David's own tribe, Judah, and the rest of Israel's tribes. This foreign-manned standing army, with its reliance on taxes and forced labor, and the central role assigned to foreigners in running the kingdom broke the traditional tribal structures; and the resentful tribes arguably found their leader in Absalom. See "David's State: The Revolution and Civil War" (in Hebrew), *Beit Mikra*, 42 (1997), pp. 315–19.

27. The uses of the Ark as a fetishized object, carried along with the baggage trains of the army as a way to force God's direct participation in battle (regardless of the moral and religious standing of those who aim to instrumentalize the Ark as a weapon of war), is a central theme at the beginning of the Book of Samuel. In 1 Sam 4–6, the author critically explores the fetish problem in relation to the demise of the corrupt lineage of the priests. Later, when David attempted to bring the ark to Jerusalem, he too was taught the dangers of attempting to recruit the ark as a legitimating political tool; this concern comes into focus in 2 Sam 6. Abravanel astutely made the following observation in his commentary: "David commanded the return of the Ark to Jerusalem since he was concerned with the Ark's honor, and he also feared that God would punish him for abusing the Ark as God did in the days of Eli when Israel brought God's Ark to war without God's command and they were punished" (2 Sam 2:15, p. 364).

28. David's humility is expressed by the fact that, when he imagines a possible atonement and restoration, he mentions finding favor in the eyes of God who "will bring me back and let me see it and its abode" (2 Sam 15:25). As Bar-Efrat notes in his commentary (p. 169), no mention is made of a return to full control and power, but rather solely of mending his standing before God. It is also interesting to note a reversal implicit in the narrative: in the story of the killing of Uriah, David stayed in Jerusalem while the Ark was on the move with the

army in the field; but this time David is forced to leave the city while the Ark remains in Jerusalem.

29. In 2 Sam 21, we are told that David handed the two sons of Rizpah, Saul's concubine, and the five sons of Merab, Saul's legitimate daughter and Michal's elder sister, to be killed by the Gibeonites in order to appease them. This chapter is rightfully regarded by scholars as an appendix to the book rather than an integral part of the narrative that we are analyzing. As a result, the extent to which these events contributed to the anger of the Saulides as described in our narrative remains uncertain.

30. Abishai is portrayed here as true to himself, befitting the tension developed throughout the narrative between Joab's and Abishai's brand of power politics and David's far more sophisticated approach to achieving and maintaining power. This encounter thus reminds us of David's refusal to allow Abishai to murder the defenseless Saul (1 Sam 26:8–9) just as he here refuses to allow Abishai to murder Shimei who was pleading for forgiveness (2 Sam 19:22–24). For a different evaluation of David, Abishai, and Shimei in these verses see, Timothy F. Simpson, "Not 'Who IS on the Lord's Side?' but 'Whose Side Is the Lord On?': Contesting Claims and Divine Inscrutability," in "2 Samuel 16:5–14," *Studies in Biblical Literature* vol. 152 (New York: Peter Lang Publishing, 2014) pp. 53–92.

31. Polzin notes that David, in verse 12, employs the same verb "heshiv" (translated by Alter as "to requite") also used by Shimei in his curse: "The LORD has brought back (heshiv) upon you." On the importance of this verb throughout the narrative, see Polzin, *David and the Deuteronomist* (pp. 156–58).

32. Here, as always with David, the moral-religious dimension is intertwined with political calculus. It might be that David thought that killing Shimei, a member of Saul's clan, would open up another front for him at a moment of vulnerability and would also alienate the tribe of Benjamin by confirming his irreconcilable hostility to the house of Saul. David's eventual deathbed order to put Shimei to death, although it might possibly signal a change of heart, could also demonstrate that already in this initial encounter David was motivated by political expediency in not retaliating against Shimei, so that when such leniency no longer brought palpable political advantage, he felt free to have Shimei killed. On this issue, see our concluding chapter.

33. Focusing on Ahitophel's words, "and the hand of all who are with you will be strengthened" (2 Sam 16:21), Rashi makes the following point: "Now they are hesitant in supporting you since they say in their heart 'the son will reconcile with his father and we will become the king's enemies'" (2 Sam 16:21).

34. Shimon Bar-Efrat presents a meticulous literary reading of the rhetorical force of Hushai's speech in *Narrative Art in the Bible* (Sheffield: Sheffield Academic Press, 1989), pp. 223–37.

35. Mishnah Sotah 1, 8.

36. Here again, killing through subordinate agents is a mark of power; recall that Absalom himself killed Amnon by commanding his lads (young servants) to do the deed (2 Sam 13:28–29).

37. The narrative makes use of the term "shalom" (all is well) in order to heighten David's acute concern for his son. The messenger Ahimaaz began his statement with "Shalom!" ("All is well") (2 Sam 18: 28). David, on the other hand, was concerned with the well-being of one subject—his son—and he responded to the message with the following question: "ha-shalom la-na'ar Abshalom" ("is it well with the lad Absalom") (2 Sam 18:29). As Alter notes, the word shalom is the last part of Absalom's name in Hebrew. There is also a bitter irony in the fact that the first syllable of Absalom (Avshalom) relates to the father ("Av").

38. Levi ben Gershon (Ralbag) makes the following astute point concerning David's guilt: "And David cried in this exceptional way over the death of Absalom since he knew that the death was caused by his own transgressions" (Ralbag on 2 Sam 19:1).

39. The ruler's power, as this episode makes clear, depends on the undying and nonstrategic loyalty of his troops. This is why Joab defines David's mistake not as sacrificing warmhearted love to coldhearted power but as loving those who hate you and hating those who love you (2 Sam 19:7). By interweaving state structures with the king's intimate family, dynastic monarchy sets the stage for a fatal clash between the king's sentimental and indulgent attachment to his male heirs and the absolute necessity of retaining the uncalculating allegiance of his military followers. This is what we mean by the clash between the logic of love and the logic of power.

40. Bar-Efrat notes that Joab addressed the king with no deference, completely out of line with the manners of the court (commentary on II, 19:6, p. 201). In speaking this way, Joab communicated to David how much of his soldiers' respect he had lost. Joab's threat to abandon the king and desert with the rest of the army was real. Indeed, his defection was imminent. Rather than pleading with the king, he commanded him in a curt sequence of orders: "And now, rise, go out, and speak to the heart of your servants" (2 Sam 19:8).

41. Jan Fokkelman astutely analyzed the gap between Joab's order and David's feeble performance; see *Narrative Art and Poetry in the Books of Samuel,* vol. 1, p. 274.

42. Absalom's rebellion, having exposed David's deteriorating grip on power, was followed by another rebellion by a Benjaminite leader,

Sheba son of Bichri, against David, a rebellion narrated in 2 Sam 20. This second rebellion was crushed by Joab who, while achieving victory, also managed to kill Amasa, who had been chosen by David to replace Joab as the leader of the army sent to fight the rebellion. David might possibly have picked Amasa as the new leader of his army, even though he had led Absalom's army of rebellion, in order to reconcile with the principal supporters of Absalom's rebellion. In addition, the replacement of Joab by Amasa might have been motivated by David's need to punish Joab somehow for his killing of Absalom.

CHAPTER 4: DAVID'S WILL AND LAST WORDS

1. That our author wants us to see Adonijah's brazen grab for the throne as a direct result of David's lifelong pampering of his male children is stressed by Mordechai Cogan, *I Kings*, in *The Anchor Bible* (New York: Doubleday, 2001), p. 157.

2. Ralbag, among other medieval commentators, pointed to Joab's interest in supporting Adonijah: "And Joab was drawn to Adonijah and supported his scheme to become the monarch in order that he will love him and will not depose him from his role as the commander of the army, since it was clear to him that David intended to depose him from his rank because of what happened with Absalom" (1 Kgs 1:7).

3. Jan Fokkelman suggests that the narrator stresses David's inaction and passivity by the use of the verb yad'a—to know. David didn't have sexual intercourse with Abishag: "The king knew her not" (1 Kgs 1:4), nor was he aware of Adonijah's plot as Nathan said: "and our lord David knows it not" (1 Kgs 1:11). Impotence and ignorance are here tied together. *Narrative Art and Poetry in the Books of Samuel*, vol.. 1, p. 350.

4. Some commentators raise doubts about whether this oath was ever sworn since, as Alter points out in his annotations (1 Kgs 1:13, p. 366), no such vow was mentioned in the prior narrative. This omission opens the possibility that Nathan, in order to secure Solomon's succession, was turning the tables on an inveterate dissimulator, exploiting David's aging condition to implant by power of suggestion a made-up oath that the dying king had once purportedly sworn. See as well R. N. Whybray, *The Succession Narrative*, p. 40; and David Gunn, *The Story of King David: Genre and Interpretation*, pp. 105–6.

5. This was also the aim of the statement Bathsheba made while addressing David: "And you, my lord the king, the eyes of all Israel are upon you to tell them who will sit on the throne of my lord the king after him" (1 Kgs 1:20).

6. See Alter's convincing comment on 1 Kings 2:3–4 (p. 374).

7. McKenzie empties this question of any significance, arguing that David's waiting for more than thirty years to punish Joab for killing Abner means that he could not, in fact, have wished it on his deathbed. He believes that nothing can be learned from I Kings 2:1–11 about the moral psychology of dynastic monarchy, therefore, because he reads the entire last will and testament as mere royal propaganda concocted by Solomon's spin doctors who wished to attribute the bloody beginning of Solomon's reign to David's final instructions. Steven L. McKenzie, *King David: A Biography*, pp. 178–79. For the contrary claim that David's will was intended by our author not only as a genuine lesson in statecraft, delivered from father to son, but also as David's last act of statecraft, meant to "protect Solomon against the accusation of paying off personal scores," see J. Robinson's commentary to 1 Kings 2:1–4 in *The First Book of Kings* (Cambridge: Cambridge University Press, 1972), p. 38.

8. The possibility that the murder of Amasa, an insubordinate general and defector who had just conducted a disastrously losing military campaign, served not only Joab's personal ambitions but also David's deeper dynastic interests is raised by Baruch Halpern, *David's Secret Demons*, pp. 90–91, 371.

9. Consistent with the decision to leave the motives of his characters tantalizingly ambiguous, the author here opens up the possibility that Bathsheba's agreement to act on Adonijah's behalf was motivated by her awareness that his audacious request provided the perfect opportunity to remove him from the scene. See Alter's comment on 1 Kings 2:18 (p. 378). Fokkelman (vol. 1, p. 395) points to a subtle difference in Bathsheba's presentation. Adonijah used the following language in addressing Bathsheba: "And now, there is one petition I ask of you, do not refuse me" (1 Kgs 2:16). When Bathsheba conveyed Adonijah's request to Solomon she reformulated slightly Adonijah's language: "There is one small petition that I ask of you, do not refuse me" (1 Kgs 2:20). The addition of the word "small" might be an expression of Bathsheba's desire to assist Adoniajah as Fokkelman claims, or it might point to an even greater savviness on the part of Bathsheba, who may have wished to provoke Solomon's fury by pretending Adonijah's request was a small matter.

10. Rosenberg remarks, along he same lines, that this is how the throne is "secured." Joel Rosenberg, *King and Kin. Political Allegory in the Hebrew Bible* (Bloomington: Indiana University Press, 1986), p. 187.

11. In running to seek asylum at the altar, Joab incriminated himself as well. The Septuagint version adds the following conversation to the text: "Solomon sent the message to Joab: 'What have you done, fleeing like that to the altar?' Joab said: 'because I fear you, I have fled to

the LORD.' Thereupon Solomon sent Beniah." As Fokkelman claims, this added exchange is too explicit, and diverges from the subtlety of the text as it appears in the Masoretic version. See, *Narrative Art and Poetry in the Books of Samuel* vol. 1, p. 399, note 15.

12. Adonijah's introduction to his request to Bathsheba—"You yourself know that mine was the kingship and to me did all Israel turn their faces to be king" (1 Kgs 2:13)—discloses the blind pretentiousness and pathetic feebleness of his ploy. How could he assume that Bathsheba shares that sort of self-indulgent judgment? It should have been clear to him that she was aware of the fact that if he had become the king then Solomon, her son, would have been killed. Formulating Adonijah's self-presentation in this manner is the author's way of revealing that a residual ambition for the crown still haunted the defeated prince. While Adonijah wished to present a case for compensation he was, at the same time, revealing his unsated ambition.

13. Abravanel makes the point that David's initial pardon of Shimei was motivated by David's desire to reconcile with the Benjamite constituency, emphasizing the fact that when Shimei appealed to David for forgiveness after he had defeated Absalom, Shimei arrived with a company of one thousand Benjamites: "When Shimei saw that Absalom died and David was returning to Jerusalem, he was worried that he will be punished for his cursing of the king and therefore he approached him to ask for atonement and forgiveness and he brought with him a thousand men from Benjamin and Ziba his sons and slaves, so that David will be afraid to punish him since he will make all of them his enemies" (Abravanel, 2 Sam 19: 18, p. 374) and see as well Abravanel's comment on 1 Kings 2:8, p. 499.

CONCLUSION

1. The literary conceit that the Book of Samuel represents an attempt to cover up David's dark motives and darker deeds, central to the entertaining historical novel by Stefan Heym, *The King David Report* (New York: Putnam, 1973), shipwrecks on the totally explicit and unsqueamish way in which the Samuel author dramatizes the distinction between justification and motivation, indispensable to the book's view of the exercise of sovereign authority. The same comment applies to the scholarly book by Baruch Halpern cited in footnote 4 to the Introduction.

2. On the changing conception of God's intervention in history as reflected in the "Succession Narrative," see Gerhard von Rad, *The Problem of the Hexateuch and Other Essays*, translated by E. W. Trueman Dicken (London: SCM Press, 1984), pp. 196–204.

3. To say that, for the ruler, power becomes an end-in-itself is somewhat misleading, admittedly, when the purpose of his clinging to power includes avoiding being put to death. In this sense, the kings of ancient Israel continued to view sovereign power instrumentally, even though the purpose it served was personal and dynastic survival, not national defense. Yet the experience of wielding supreme power was and remains psychologically addictive, potentially making the loss of supreme authority feel like a dissolving of personal identity. The emotional-moral identification of the ruler with the power he wields is what we have in mind when we say that sovereignty, which the people accept as a means for collective defense, easily becomes an end-in-itself for those who exercise it.

Index